MPAVILION
ENCOUNTERS WITH DESIGN
AND ARCHITECTURE

How to desi␣
Pavilion

ACKNOWLEDGEMENT OF COUNTRY

MPavilion is an annual temporary building constructed in Melbourne's Queen Victoria Gardens by the Naomi Milgrom Foundation. Each MPavilion is gifted to the people of Victoria and relocated to a permanent site for the continued enjoyment of all.

The Naomi Milgrom Foundation acknowledges the Yaluk-ut Weelam as the traditional custodians of the land on which the Queen Victoria Gardens were established in the early twentieth century. Yaluk-ut Weelam means 'people of the river camp' and is connected with the coastal land at the head of Port Phillip Bay, extending from the Werribee River to Mordialloc in Victoria, Australia. The Yaluk-ut Weelam are part of the Boon Wurrung, one of the five major language groups of the greater Kulin Nation. The Foundation pays respect to the land, to the ancestors of the Yaluk-ut Weelam and their Elders—past, present and future.

The Naomi Milgrom Foundation and all associated with this publication respectfully acknowledge Australia's First People as the traditional custodians of the land on which we work and live. We recognise their continuing connection to land, water and community and celebrate their enduring presence and knowledge.

CONTENTS

FOREWORD   19
NAOMI MILGROM

INTRODUCTION   27
STEPHEN TODD

QUEEN VICTORIA GARDENS   37

2014   SEAN GODSELL   45
        SEAN GODSELL ARCHITECTS
            OPEN IMPRESSIONS
            JULIA PEYTON-JONES

2015   AMANDA LEVETE   67
        AL_A
            THE LIMITS OF ARCHITECTURE
            RORY HYDE

        DESIGN PROCESS   85

2016   BIJOY JAIN   101
        STUDIO MUMBAI
            ALL HANDS ON THE PRESENT
            ARIC CHEN

2017   REM KOOLHAAS & DAVID GIANOTTEN   121
        OMA
            THEATRICS, SPECTACLE AND THE CITY
            ELLIE STATHAKI

        ARCHITECTURAL MODELS   141

2018   CARME PINÓS   153
        ESTUDIO CARME PINÓS
        A DESIGN FOR EVERYONE
            CAROLINE ROUX

2019   GLENN MURCUTT   173
            A TABLECLOTH UNDER A WING
            FRANÇOISE FROMONOT

        A SECOND LIFE   193
        SIMON TERRILL

        CONTAINER OF IDEAS   205

        PUBLIC ENCOUNTERS   208

        COMMISSIONS   221

        COLLABORATORS   233

        ACKNOWLEDGEMENTS   242

FOREWORD

NAOMI MILGROM AO

This book marks the completion of six remarkable years of the MPavilion series, and is a celebration of what we have collectively achieved. It is, for me, a pivotal moment rather than an end point. In many ways, this compendium of thoughtful essays and striking images is part of a continuum. It reflects a philosophy of working with trusted and talented people, and giving them creative freedom to shift the dial in terms of engagement with art, architecture, design and technology. As a way of working it resonates with the concept embedded in the exhibition 'Dream the World Awake', by Belgian fashion designer Walter Van Beirendonck, which we brought to Australia in 2013. Such an approach has allowed us to create wonderful collaborations that push us at the Naomi Milgrom Foundation to explore new opportunities and reach new audiences through ambitious public–private partnerships.

The idea of MPavilion was sparked by my close friendship with Julia Peyton-Jones, co-director of London's Serpentine Gallery at the time, and through my experience of viewing the annual Serpentine Gallery Pavilions. Similarly, MPavilion offered me a chance to say something new about contemporary architecture and design in my home city, and to explore connections with people and cultural institutions in Melbourne, Australia and internationally.

I had a specific location in mind for the project for several reasons. One was practical—it was an underutilised park close to transport and Melbourne's main cultural precinct—and another was its connection to the creative heritage of the city.

I have long admired John Truscott, an Academy Award-winning film designer, artistic director and theatre designer, who directed the Melbourne International Arts Festival from 1988 to 1991. Truscott is credited with reacquainting Melburnians with their city by creating celebratory outdoor public events. His two Botanica pavilions and a Chinese teahouse sited in the Queen Victoria Gardens stayed in my memory. I wanted to honour John's legacy, and continue his spirit of community involvement and experimentation. To use this site on an annual basis required an Act of parliament. To achieve this, we were fortunate to have the support of both the City of Melbourne and the State Government of Victoria, which also partnered with my Foundation in supporting MPavilion's free annual public program.

The process of selecting MPavilion architects—visiting their studios, meeting their teams and experiencing first-hand their broader bodies of work—has been incredibly rewarding. Each commission has taken me on a different path of appreciation and understanding. I believe all architects are, at heart, problem-solvers, and while the brief to provide shelter and observe a set footprint for the structure remained a constant, the concept, materiality and form were all entirely open to interpretation. The design brief was also about capturing an emotion. The words of the Danish humanist architect Jan Gehl sum it up: "First life, then space, then building—the other way around never works."

So, when I review the connections between the six architecture practices—Sean Godsell of Sean Godsell Architects, Amanda Levete of AL_A, Bijoy Jain of Studio Mumbai, OMA's Rem Koolhaas and David Gianotten, Carme Pinós of Estudio Carme Pinós and Glenn Murcutt—I see the same shared core values, with each expressing form in their unique architectural language. This aspect is critical, as one of my Foundation's key goals is to educate and inspire by working with the most significant architectural thinkers. Over time this has created an intriguing global exchange and a network of associations as materials are investigated and skills explored, suppliers and builders engaged, technologies developed and new alliances formed.

MPavilion was conceived as a collaborative cultural laboratory; a place for debate, entertainment, education, and most importantly a place to seed and exchange ideas. We started entirely from scratch, first building the foundations and slowly, layer upon layer, gathering awareness and growing a community of local and global collaborators.

From the beginning we aimed to make MPavilion a hub for the whole city and so consulted broadly, commissioned strategically and partnered with a wide range of creative thinkers and doers as well as cultural and educational institutions. Alongside our remit to act as a catalyst for ideas comes the freedom to take risks and seek outcomes that are multi-layered and multicultural, which has liberated the program, enabling it to evolve far beyond my original imaginings.

I have reflected on what is important to me. With MPavilion we have created a utopian space that has no barriers to entry. It is without walls, entrance fee, institutional constraints or predetermined affiliations. This leaves us open to diverse levels of engagement and exciting new relationships: the event programs we deliver, the people we partner with, the architecture we enable, the employment we generate and the breadth of community engagement we achieve. Hence, with curiosity at its core, I am excited by the energy MPavilion is generating and its enormous cultural, economic and civic impact.

That each MPavilion would have a second life and be gifted to the public to become a legacy of architect-designed pavilions in the state of Victoria was always integral to our planning. This relocation to a permanent site enables the continuation and expansion of the ethos into new communities for years to come. It also means many people gain the benefits of these unique civic spaces, dreamed up by important architectural thinkers who have distilled their distinct architectural language into these jewel-box projects.

MPavilion is also part of a new model of public–private collaborative philanthropy and through it, I have set myself the task of re-engineering how the act of giving is framed. By embedding myself in the detail of the execution, caring about every detail, using my business connections and forming partnerships with government, the corporate sector and other like-minded foundations, we are able to venture into new, stimulating areas of creative excellence. I would like to thank the City of Melbourne and its councillors, specifically former Lord Mayor, Robert Doyle, current Lord Mayor, Sally Capp, director of city design, Rob Adams and former CEO, Kathy Alexander. I would also like to thank the State Government of Victoria through Creative Victoria and Development Victoria and our key corporate partner ANZ for sharing this vision.

There are many other companies, philanthropic trusts and individuals who have contributed to the success of MPavilion. Their continued and ongoing support, together with my Foundation's board and the MPavilion team have made it possible to have achieved so much over the past six years. I would like to especially thank the Minister for Creative Industries, Martin Foley MP, for his continued involvement in MPavilion and the inspiration he has taken from it to promote contemporary architecture and design in Victoria.

The last ten years have allowed me to meet some of the most interesting people on the planet and have made me more thoughtful about the planning of cities and how architecture and design touches everything—past, present and future. We have found new levels of understanding unfold as we immerse ourselves in each architect's philosophy, bringing an increasingly humanitarian aspect to everything we do.

Beyond the architects themselves, we have succeeded in drawing some of the world's most fascinating designers, artists and thinkers to MPavilion. Not only do we benefit from their insights and perspective;

they also take a deeper appreciation of our creative pulse back into their world. By fostering discussion, we are building Melbourne's international reputation while advancing the debate about the role design, architecture and culture have in developing cities that are sustainable, liveable and equitable.

MPavilion has brought me immense pride and great joy and I hope you enjoy this publication, which draws together the phenomenal creative expression that the entire endeavour represents.

Image
Naomi Milgrom and Amanda Levete
at MPavilion 2015.

"I SEE MPAV
PLACE OF E
A SPACE TO
THE ESSEN
WORLD—AND

BIJOY JAIN

ILION AS A
IGAGEMENT:
 DISCOVER
IALS OF THE
 OF ONESELF."

INTRODUCTION

STEPHEN TODD

27

"Even with the most modest architecture projects, you are changing the world."—*Rem Koolhaas and David Gianotten*

Architecture's quest for permanence, even immortality, traditionally set it at odds with the ephemeral. The temporary was considered flighty, light-weight, lacking gravitas. And yet, with increasing frequency over the past two decades, architects both renowned and relatively unknown have been testing the parameters of the temporary in pavilions dedicated to culture or commerce.

While the temporary architectural pavilion is now a transcontinental phenomenon, the purpose (or not) to which they are put, the messages they are intended to convey and the way in which they reflect and affect local populations are as diverse as the minds that conceive them.

To fully understand the MPavilions, which have variously squatted, swayed, blossomed and gleamed in Melbourne's Queen Victoria Gardens these past six years, it is necessary to understand the woman who commissioned them, and the urban context in which they've flourished.

Naomi Milgrom, entrepreneur and philanthropist, had two key objectives for the MPavilion project she established in 2014 and operates under the aegis of the foundation that bears her name.

Firstly, to erect transient structures by significant contemporary architects in order to stimulate conversations around architecture, design and the future of urban centres. The built form was not to be considered an end in itself, but as a facilitator of cultural debate.

Secondly, the pavilions would provide innovative civic space for a broad range of cultural activities for the people of Melbourne.

For its major government supporters, the City of Melbourne and the State Government of Victoria, MPavilion has been a leading voice in the promotion of the city and the state's standing as a global cultural capital and centre for design innovation. For the local design industry, MPavilion has provided a highly visible and generative forum. And for the broader community the pavilions offer thoughtful, engaging structures in an accessible parkland setting that provide a four-month long roster of free activities.

It's a safe bet that nowhere else in the world could you witness a canine costume competition under the awning of a Bijoy Jain bamboo shelter, dance in the dark beneath a canopy of translucent petals designed by Amanda Levete of A_LA, or engage in a debate about urban planning with Rem Koolhaas in a purpose-built modular ampitheatre by his studio, OMA.

Aligned with no institution, MPavilion collaborates with many. All Melbourne's universities have a place on the program, as have at various times more than one hundred different organisations including the Australian Chamber Orchestra, Multicultural Arts Victoria, Australian Institute of Architects, Melbourne Music Week, British Council, Office of the Victorian Government Architect and The Wheeler Centre for Books, Writing and Ideas.

An evolving program of talks, debates, workshops and presentations has covered everything from open source architecture to how smart data is shaping our identities, to the future of gender equality and the art of sport.

Sir Nicholas Serota, chair of Arts Council England, sees MPavilion as "part of the general phenomenon around the world where people enjoy congregating in informal situations and contexts and debating, discussing contemporary ideas. It is part of the phenomenon of encouraging people to be participants rather than simply an audience."

Image
Rem Koolhaas and David Gianotten
at MPavilion 2017

Serota presented a talk on 'the art museum in flux' within Carme Pinós's slatted timber 2018 MPavilion, which according to the architect was conceived as "a catalyst for encounters and relationships".[1]

Each of Milgrom's commissions has stemmed not just from an intellectual conviction of the significance of the architect and their body of work, but from an intuitive understanding of their importance to an ongoing dialogue about the urban condition.

"They all have a unique architectural language, they are great architects without a doubt," she says. "But it is about their humanity, their humility and the way they see architecture and design's place in the world that is so important."

A prominent fashion retailer with a background in teaching, publishing, marketing and philanthropy, over the past three decades Milgrom has sat on numerous boards in the arts, health, education and business sectors. Notably, her appointment to the inaugural board of the Melbourne Fashion Festival (launched in the late 1990s to stimulate the market but also raise awareness of fashion as a dynamic vector of cultural production) laid the ground for today's MPavilion program.

As chair of the festival and with its creative director, Robert Buckingham, Milgrom oversaw the growth of a public program of seminars, fashion events and exhibitions, mobilising her business and government contacts to create what was in effect an impactful arts, education and retail program.

The curated events calendar included fashion shows and presentations from national and international creatives, including Belgian iconoclast Walter Van Beirendonck who impressed Milgrom with the multi-disciplinarity of his design approach—and his insistence on engaging directly with fans and students.

A decade after Van Beirendonck's appearance at the festival, Milgrom and Buckingham proposed to RMIT University that an exhibition of his work might be an appropriate way to inaugurate its new RMIT Design Hub, designed by Sean Godsell, in 2013.

The enthusiasm around the 'Dream the World Awake' show—which Milgrom considers "possibly the most extraordinarily designed exhibition Melbourne has ever seen"—was thrilling. But even more exciting was being able to plug Van Beirendonck into the university's teaching program, to have him work with fashion and design students and influence the direction of RMIT's fashion design curriculum.

"That's the way I like to do things," says Milgrom. "I like to enable links, to build on ideas to give them greater capacity in the community."

As Van Beirendonck's exhibition drew to a close, Milgrom began thinking of ways to keep that energy alive, to extend the lessons learnt during the extremely successful activation of the RMIT Design Hub.

Conversations with her long-standing friend and ally, Julia Peyton-Jones, director of London's Serpentine Gallery from 1991 to 2016, convinced Milgrom that an annual architectural pavilion for Melbourne would provide an ideal forum for ongoing discussions about the vital role of the creative industries in a city often heralded as one of the world's most liveable.

The Naomi Milgrom Foundation was established in 2014 as a framework within which Milgrom could consolidate her design-related philanthropic activities, particularly through the creation of the MPavilion program.

From the beginning, she had a set of non-negotiables. Entry to MPavilion and all its activities were to be free and the project would be a joint public–private venture with the support of the city and the state government. It would reject parochialism and seek the involvement of leading architectural and design thinkers from Australia and around the

1
Caroline Roux on Carme Pinós
    Image
Virgina Trioli, Rem Koolhaas, David Gianotten
and Naomi Milgrom at MPavilion 2017.

world. Once each summer's program was over, Milgrom would gift the pavilion to the city for permanent installation at a location to be decided on a case-by-case basis.

Most doggedly, she insisted that there was only one possible location for the MPavilions to be installed each summer: in the Queen Victoria Gardens opposite the capital's major cultural precinct along the arterial St Kilda Road just before it crosses the Yarra River and feeds into the grid of downtown Melbourne.

* * *

The first British settlement in Australia was in 1788 with the arrival of the First Fleet in Sydney. The city of Melbourne, however, was not established until 1835 when settlers from Tasmania appropriated the lands of the Kulin Nation and began the process of displacing the original inhabitants. When gold was discovered in the new colony of Victoria in the 1850s, Melbourne grew rapidly—becoming for a time the wealthiest city in the world—and has a significant Victorian architectural heritage as a result. Charles La Trobe, the first colonial supervisor of the area, is largely responsible for planning Melbourne as a city surrounded by parks, establishing public reserves around the city, including the 36-hectare Kings Domain in 1854. A corner of this area which had been prone to flooding was redeveloped into a park as a memorial to Queen Victoria upon her death in 1901, the year of Australian Federation.

Featuring statues of the British monarchs, rose gardens and a floral clock set amidst verdant lawns and European trees, the Queen Victoria Gardens were layered onto the history of contested ownership; the 4.8-hectare park is a palimpsest of Australia's colonial heritage

With the opening of the Roy Grounds-designed National Gallery of Victoria on St Kilda Road in 1968 and his masterplanning of a new arts precinct opposite the gardens, Melbourne's leafy arterial avenue attained a new vitality. But it was John Truscott who would really bring the nascent art precinct to life.

Truscott, who died in 1993, is a titan of Melbourne's cultural mythology. A stage actor of some talent, it was as a production and costume designer that he truly shined, scoring an Academy Award in each category for his gargantuan undertaking on Joshua Logan's 1967 Hollywood extravaganza, *Camelot*. Returning to Melbourne, in the late 1970s he was commissioned to design the interiors of the new Concert Hall and State Theatre, adjacent to the National Gallery of Victoria. And from 1988 to 1991 he was the creative director of what would become the Melbourne International Arts Festival, a program of public events that brought cultural production—something hitherto thought as only for the elite—to the community at large.

Some remember the archways Truscott had constructed as celebratory entrances to the city along St Kilda Road. Others recall the thousands of paper lanterns hung throughout the avenue's trees, or the Chinese teahouse and botanic pavilions temporarily installed in the Queen Victoria Gardens. Almost all who experienced them reminisce on Truscott's creative genius and his commitment to turning the city's elegant assets over to what in those days were still referred to as 'the masses'.

For Milgrom, positioning the MPavilions along a continuum was a means of inscribing them into the history—and future—of the city. That it required an Act of parliament in order for her to use the site is only testimony to her temerity.

Originally planned as a three-year exercise, the success of the first MPavilion meant that by the time the second was being planned, all stakeholders—including state and municipal government, tertiary

Image
King Edward VII statue (1920) and Floral Clock (1966), Queen Victoria Gardens, Melbourne, Australia.

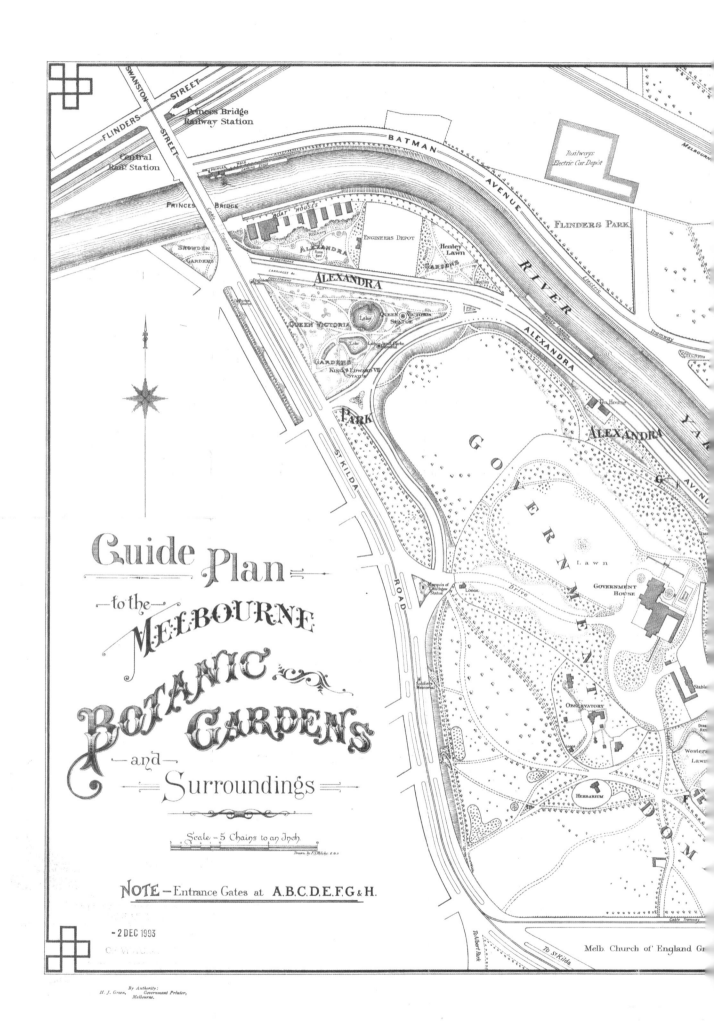

Guide Plan
to the
MELBOURNE
BOTANIC GARDENS
and
Surroundings

Scale — 5 Chains to an Inch.

Drawn by F.S.Blake, F.M.I.

NOTE — Entrance Gates at A.B.C.D.E.F.G & H.

– 2 DEC 1993

H. J. Green,   By Authority:
Government Printer,
Melbourne.

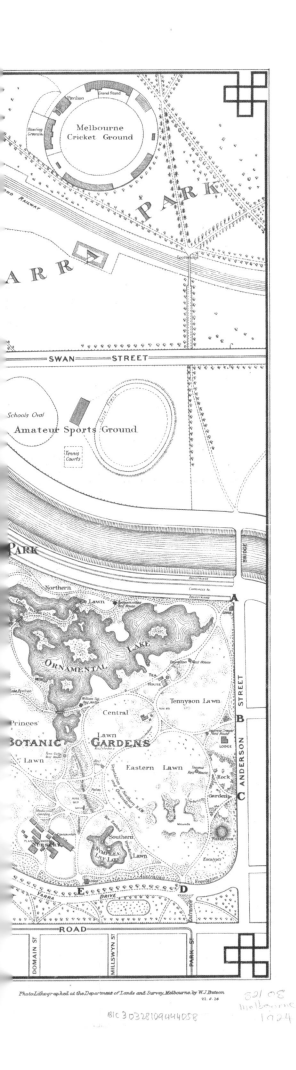

Botanic Gardens: Queen Victoria Gardens,
Alexandra Park, 1924.
Drawn by F.S. Hilke dated 6.10.1911.
State Library of Victoria Pictures Collection.

institutes and private enterprise—as well as Milgrom herself became convinced that the program should be extended to five years, then six. At the time of publication, MPavilion is confirmed to run at least another two years, to 2022.

But the pavilions are endowed with a second life since they are gifted to the city, to cultural institutions or educational bodies. OMA's ampitheatre MPavilion now sits on the lawns at Monash University. Bijoy Jain's bamboo structure holds pride of place at the Melbourne Zoo, and A_LA's petal canopied MPavilion sways in the breeze in the Docklands district.

"When it was first installed, the Docklands site was still being developed," explains Professor Robert Adams, director of city design and projects at the City of Melbourne, "but Levete's pavilion has created a focal point for the community and green space has grown up around it in a way which feels organic."

In fact, the MPavilions are an intrinsic part of the planned redevelopment of inner Melbourne set in place in the early 1980s and still in train today. Post-WWII suburban expansion had turned the capital of Victoria into a "donut city"—substantial on the periphery, empty in the middle—and new state and local governments were determined to reverse that trend. Not by attempting to change the nature of downtown (referred to in Australia, tellingly, as the central business district, or CBD) but by enhancing existing attributes they identified as quintessentially Melbourne: the boulevards, parks, arcades and laneways established in the nineteenth century.

Adams, who was engaged at the time by the city as part of a small team to devise an urban design strategy, has been responsible for its delivery ever since—and that continuity has formed the backbone of what is often referred to as 'the Melbourne Miracle'.

Since the majority of innovation was fine-grained and long-term, incremental to the point of almost imperceptible, the council commissioned Danish urbanist Jan Gehl to help track the panoply of changes in what would become the 1994 Places for People report and form the benchmark by which progress would be judged in a second report a decade later and a third in 2015.

Melbourne, today a city of some five million people (and expected to hit eight million by 2050) now boasts a 24-hour downtown, laneways alive with cafés, bars and small businesses, and stretches across the river where a bankside promenade anchors a vibrant restaurant precinct. Plans for a $1 billion development of the arts precinct will consolidate several existing—and provide the framework for more—cultural facilities and produce the foundation for a new neighbourhood.

From the Queen Victoria Gardens, with views across the river back to the Melbourne skyline, each MPavilion has existed in symbiosis with the city's development. In a sense, the eclecticism of the selection echoes the exuberance of the city itself, with its Victorian foundations famously interspersed with a grab bag of buildings of almost every 20th century architectural movement with a particularly fine showing of what might be termed antipodean post-modernism.

As Ellie Stathaki writes in her essay on OMA's 2017's MPavilion, by addressing the structure as a key piece in Melbourne's urban fabric, "the architects explore the overall form not as a self-containing piece, but as a part of the city's overall current dynamic."[2]

Of course, temporary pavilions have engendered criticism. Neither building nor sculpture, the hybridity of pavilions tends to rile rivals on both sides. And as temporary architectural structures have become fashionable it's easy to dismiss them as an empty trend, or as manifestations of the 'festivilification' of culture.

2
Ellie Stathaki on Rem Koolhaas and David Gianotten.
Image
MPavilion 2019.

Image
MPavilion 2017 at Monash University,
Clayton campus.

In the case of the MPavilion, particularly the fact that significant urban interventions are the result of a single, private commissioner could be seen as problematic. As could the fact that those commissions are often awarded to overseas practices, thereby diverting potential patronage from local creatives.

Milgrom, while a proud Melburnian, is also an avowed internationalist. A member of the Art Basel Global Patrons Council and Tate Museum London's International Council, she was Australia's commissioner for the 2017 Venice Biennale. Her will is to create meaningful dialogue and impact locally, nationally and internationally, to build a potent platform that will allow conversations to resonate beyond their physical setting.

To further the dialogue and debate generated by MPavilion, since 2017 the Naomi Milgrom Foundation has facilitated an annual Living Cities Forum held in Melbourne each winter. A three-day workshop, the forum brings together thought-leaders in the fields of design, architecture and urban planning to reflect on means to make accessible, equitable and generous cities. In this context, for instance, Carme Pinós and Nicholas Lobo Brennan have presented frameworks for housing diversity and social exchange; Liam Young and Saskia Sassen have revealed some of the larger forces that shape contemporary life.

Where the MPavilion, held at the start of Australia's summer, is the heart of Milgrom's ambition, the wintry Living Cities Forum is the mind. Together they have reinforced Melbourne's profile as a vibrant city and its role as a vital ideas incubator, ensuring it a place in the ongoing global debate about the way we live now, and into the future.

On the local level, the MPavilion program has contributed significantly to an understanding of architecture and design as powerful drivers of the culture and of the economy.

According to the Victorian Minister for Creative Industries, Martin Foley, "MPavilion has become one of Australia's most significant architectural and design projects, playing a leading role in celebrating and promoting good design and sparking a public conversation about its value. Whilst Naomi will no doubt say its success is due to collaboration and partnership—her leadership and passion have seen design and design principles now occupy a central place in our civic thinking."

Or, as Rem Koolhaas put it during a talk at the OMA-designed MPavilion in October 2017, the civic pavilion is "a tool for you to discuss the future of your city ... to discover another culture and to be active in another culture. MPavilion is such a small intervention in Melbourne, a city of nearly five million people, but plays such a huge role in the community."

Stephen Todd is a writer, editor and creative director with some thirty years' experience in the design sector. Based in Sydney, Australia, he is the design editor of the *Australian Financial Review* newspaper and creative director of Sydney Design Week.

Image
Minsuk Cho at Living Cities Forum 2017.

QUEEN VICTORIA GARDENS

SENSE OF PLACE

37

QUEEN VICTORIA GARDENS

p. 38
Queen Victoria Gardens.
p. 39
Queen Victoria Memorial (1907).
p. 40
Farnese Hercules (installed 1928).
p. 41
Lady Janet Clarke Memorial (1913).
p. 42
Queen Victoria Gardens.
p. 43
King Edward VII statue (1920).

Photography: John Betts.

MPAVILION 2014
SEAN GODSELL
SEAN GODSELL
ARCHITECTS

OPEN IMPRESSIONS
DAME JULIA PEYTON-JONES OBE
WITH SEAN GODSELL

JULIA PEYTON-JONES
What do you think MPavilion does that other architecture commissions don't do or can't do?

SEAN GODSELL
Projects like MPavilion introduce the work of an architect to an area whose population may not otherwise be familiar with that person's work. MPavilion also reintroduces into the discussion the role of the patron in architecture and that has a long and interesting history. You guys in Britain started it all: to draw a link between the Pagoda in Kew Gardens in London and the MPavilion in Queen Victoria Gardens in Melbourne isn't such a long bow.

JULIA PEYTON-JONES
Of course MPavilion is a temporary structure in the gardens and, like the Serpentine Gallery Pavilion in London, it also has a life after its display in the park, which is a fantastic idea.

SEAN GODSELL
That fantastic idea is a very hard architectural problem. Normally, we can build and assume that our buildings are going to be there for thousands of years, so the problem of making and then unmaking and then remaking is more complex. There's a lot of important stuff in a building that we don't see: all the foundations in the ground that support the bit we do see. In the case of a temporary pavilion, it goes against this. Normally, one doesn't, in my view, want to be thinking of assembly and disassembly rather than the permanence of the structure because that makes the whole thing a little bit transient.

JULIA PEYTON-JONES
For the Serpentine Gallery Pavilion, the model wasn't one of architecture, but one of exhibitions and the idea that if exhibitions can travel, so can the pavilion. And we always found that reinstalling the pavilions after they were bought was as labour-intensive as it was to build them in the first place. The materials needed to be more permanent and the idea of sustainability and robustness was an element that needed to be taken into consideration, whereas when the commission was first unveiled, that wasn't an issue because it was a very short-term problem.

SEAN GODSELL
It's the initial problem and cost—and then to make it possible to take it away and do it all again somewhere else has a hidden extra cost and problems that come with it.

JULIA PEYTON-JONES
Are there other inherent challenges in designing a temporary structure like MPavilion?

SEAN GODSELL
It depends on the particular problem you're interrogating in your structure—whether it is, in the case of my MPavilion, the idea of a kinetic façade, or in the case of Amanda Levete's pavilion, an investigation into new material. And provided the project's patron is prepared to support the architect's agenda then who knows what might come from that interrogation? That's actually a really nice component of these projects.

JULIA PEYTON-JONES
The 2014 MPavilion was very much part of your architectural language. It was a natural progression that had a very strong relationship to your work. Is that how you also see it, with the benefit of hindsight?

SEAN GODSELL
Oh yes, for me that's very normal. Every architect has a different methodology. Mine is to find an idea, articulate the idea and then rearticulate it over a series of projects until I feel I've thoroughly investigated it. My MPavilion came from a tiny alteration to a workers cottage where I needed to get light into the terraced house and the only way I could do it was through the roof. So the animated roofscape from that project made its way into the MPavilion. Our recently completed House in the Hills has another interpretation of the same idea. So, that's the way I work: I like to go over and over and over the idea until I've thoroughly investigated it, at least to my satisfaction—and then I look elsewhere.

JULIA PEYTON-JONES
And do you feel that your MPavilion was quintessentially Australian? For me, context is everything in architecture.

SEAN GODSELL
My MPavilion incorporates a romantic vision of the Outback and of the reality of the pioneers in Australia. Our history is one of adversity. In Australia, shade on a forty-degree day is the difference between life and death. If you're caught in the Outback with no shade, you're probably going to die unless someone finds you and rescues you. And most Australian architects have a deeply imbedded belief that anything constructed in Australia can represent safety and salvation from the elements, from the things here that can kill you so quickly, and so that manifests itself in our day-to-day. Hay sheds and barns and outbuildings in the remote parts of Australia sit on the horizon quite dramatically as man-made interventions into the landscape. The hay shed is a very crude way of describing a sophisticated parasol that provides shade, so that's where it was coming from with the MPavilion.

I think a mistake architects often make with these kinds of commissions is that they try to put too much architecture into the architecture and they end up with very contorted, what I call 'desperately interesting' small buildings. The MPavilion is effectively a parasol with a simple, classical plan.

JULIA PEYTON-JONES
The nature of any pavilion is so simple and it doesn't leave much room for complication. However, if the shed doesn't offer any difference of experience to a visitor, then the danger is that it's boring. So the fact that your façade was elegant, balletic and moved like a fan was incredibly important.

SEAN GODSELL

What I did was to trick people into believing that it might be really boring and to create a completely abstract object that has no obvious architectural articulation and then to undo that preconception by animating the façade. That's where the poetry in that project is—in the fact that one's expectations are lowered by the apparent banality of the box and then raised beyond belief by the fact that the box isn't quite what it appeared to be on first impression. And that's the really simple trick in architecture.

JULIA PEYTON-JONES

Well, you say it's simple. I'm not sure that all architects would agree!

SEAN GODSELL

Well, yes [laughs].

JULIA PEYTON-JONES

Let's say, in principle, it's simple. That simplicity is a fantastic strength in your MPavilion.

SEAN GODSELL

It's about getting onto the knife edge really quickly and being prepared to go there, and knowing that you're going to fall on the right side of the edge. I said to Naomi Milgrom—because we hadn't worked together at that stage—I said, "Architecture is a leap of faith. You've got to hold my hand. We're going to run to the edge of the cliff. We're going to jump and fly. You've got to trust me that everything I do will give you a dramatic outcome. You'll get architecture, but it won't on first cut appear that way. It may appear uninteresting to you. You've got to hang in there while we make it something dramatic." And that is architecture, really. It is reasonable to describe my MPavilion as a piece of classicism like Bramante's Tempietto de la San Pietro in Rome or an ancient Greek hypostyle hall. There's a lot of stuff invested into what is apparently quite simple. It is not light-hearted architecture at all.

JULIA PEYTON-JONES

Your references are always fascinating and complex. Did you talk to any of your colleagues about the scheme and how you might deal with the challenges of your proposal before you submitted it?

SEAN GODSELL

Well, in my office my associate Hayley Franklin and I always debate and argue the project. Hayley has an extremely well-trained and good eye and she is not afraid to critique and comment. We always like to do multiple schemes for any project—our design process is iterative and inclusive. We had two different schemes for the MPavilion before the one that was ultimately built. The first was a truncated conical structure, which Naomi didn't like, which was fine. We threw that one in the bin.

Then we had a variation on Peter Zumthor's Serpentine Pavilion in 2011, which has, as you well know, a beautiful Piet Oudolf internal garden. I had a circular version of that, so it was like a doughnut. I didn't like that one, but I felt I was getting closer to providing Naomi with what she was imagining as a performance venue. We threw that out as well. Then I started thinking, "What are we really doing and how are we representing the architecture of Australia and the history of Australia in a very simple structure?" I think it's a normal part of the design process to conceive and then reject schemes. Any architect who says they get a flash of genius and then miraculously produce a building is probably lying!

JULIA PEYTON-JONES

Yes, I'm sure. Creation is an evolutive process and it was ever thus. But it's interesting that your MPavilion doesn't have a verandah. I'm not saying that it should have done, but the verandah is quintessentially Australian and is also something that's evident in a lot of your work.

SEAN GODSELL

Well, I would say that on a certain level the MPavilion is a verandah. It's the abstracted version of a verandah that we first started looking at way back around the turn of the century when we did a house called the Carter Tucker House, which is a three-level beach house surrounded by horizontal timber batons that open. When I wrote about that building twenty years ago, I started talking about the abstracted verandah and the fluid nature of verandahs as architectural space. In functional terms, verandahs are unprogrammed. In the traditional Australian Outback house, they're adapted so that they might be enclosed in part: you might dine on the verandah in the evening; you might sleep out on the veranda in hot weather and so on. So they become dynamic spaces. And then the interest in how to represent that dynamism in an abstract way is where that simple first idea came from. So I would accept an argument that the MPavilion is actually a verandah.

JULIA PEYTON-JONES

I always think of verandahs as being attached to a larger building, which is probably my misunderstanding of the term. You could say the essence of a verandah is the idea of a space being revealed, which you constructed brilliantly in the MPavilion, with the lifting of the 'arms'.

SEAN GODSELL

It's the awning, the overhang. When the British first came to Australia they built Georgian houses that were completely inappropriate for hot climates. They did that in India, Africa and America as well. The addition of the verandah on a Georgian house is really the history of the colonial house. In hot climates they were used to create cooler transition spaces between inside and outside. So they're perfect environmental design devices, but they also have all this other abstract potential. We are so often briefed to provide rooms of a certain size and shape, so to suddenly find a ribbon of space wrapping around the building is interesting. Other possibilities emerge. Verandahs also become secondary circulation spaces. Those same Georgian houses had central corridors with rooms on either side of the corridor, but suddenly, with the addition of a verandah, you could access a room from the outside perimeter space. Interestingly, the verandah in the traditional Japanese house is a completely different thing in a completely different culture, but it has the same impact and effect.

JULIA PEYTON-JONES

There are many wonderful things about your MPavilion, and one of them is that it was open, it wasn't prescriptive, so performances and film screenings, discussions and debates could all take place in it, but you didn't walk in and think, "There's nothing happening here, I've come at the wrong time." Were the events that took place in the pavilion very much part of your thinking?

SEAN GODSELL

Yes, they were, but at the same time, as the first architect commissioned to design the MPavilion, we were kind of the guinea pig project for Naomi. I think her agenda and her programming have evolved and have probably become more sophisticated and fine-tuned now, and so I imagine she is briefing architects with more particular requirements. Because we were the first cab in the rank, we tried to be everything to everybody in terms of the potential for the building to work as a performance space. I think we kind of got it close to right. The ability to open up and close down the elements was considered useful. With the exception of Amanda's MPavilion, the other pavilions have become amphitheatre-like in their design, with static roofs and theatre seating. Our pavilion was clearly nothing like that.

Dame Julia Peyton-Jones DBE is the senior global director at Galerie Thaddaeus Ropac in London, Paris and Salzburg. Julia is formerly the director and co-director of exhibitions and programmes of London's Serpentine Galleries, commissioning its annual Serpentine Gallery Pavilion. In 2014, Julia joined Naomi Milgrom AO and Sean Godsell to launch the MPavilion project in Melbourne.

MPavilion 2014 was gifted by the Naomi Milgrom Foundation to the people of Victoria and relocated to the Hellenic Museum in Melbourne in 2015. The building has since been significantly modified by the museum.

p. 52–63
Photography: Earl Carter.
p. 64–65
Photography: Courtesy MPavilion.

MPAVILION 2015

AMANDA LEVETE
AL_A

THE LIMITS OF ARCHITECTURE
DR RORY HYDE

What are the limits of architecture? When does it become so ephemeral that it threatens to drift away? What if the pieces are so peculiar that they can't be built by regular means? What if the ideas that shape it have little grounding in history? These are the questions posed by AL_A's MPavilion. A structure so light and transparent as to be barely there, and yet one which can ultimately point toward a new path for architecture's future.

As you approach, AL_A's pavilion doesn't so much appear as come into focus. A cluster of slender black rods, with shifting white shingles above, the pavilion is almost as insubstantial as is physically possible. There are no walls, and the timber floor is at ground level, continuous with the surrounding lawn. With no clear edge to enclose an interior, it is ambiguous where it begins and ends. The thin white petals which form the roof, could barely be called a roof at all, more of a cloud or field. This is architecture at its most disembodied. Barely there, and yet at the same time, undoubtedly, there.

The pavilion is a particular challenge for architects. At once expected to be a manifesto, to capture the essence of a practice, but also to be an experiment, to express new research and ideas, unburdened from the demands of 'real' building. "It's a very difficult thing to design a pavilion," Amanda Levete CBE explains, "precisely because it's not a building. When I think of a pavilion, I think of a park, I think of a bandstand, I think of something a bit temporary. I don't think of the folly. I think of it as a piece of landscape, or something between the two."

Originally sited within Melbourne's Domain Parklands, Levete's inspiration was the surrounding clusters of trees. "A tree canopy is a place that you naturally go to for shelter and shade," Levete says. "People always gravitate towards this kind of shelter, whether it's from the sun, the wind or the rain. It's a kind of human instinct." Like a tree canopy, the pavilion is not separated from the weather, but merely filters it, providing cover, while letting the wind blow through, admitting drops of rain, and dappled sun. "I liked the idea of creating a structure that would respond to the weather, that would gently sway in the wind, and almost dematerialise at its edges," Levete explains. "A structure that would feel very settled within this parkland context."

But far from being 'natural', Levete's forest canopy is forged from cutting-edge technology. Made of black carbon fibre and clear white resin, these are materials rarely found in a forest, nor in architecture for that matter. "As architects, we look at nature, and it's almost done. The complexity, the beauty, the diversity. It's impossible to beat it," Levete says. "The challenge, then, is to use completely man-made technology, man-made materials, and invest it with something that feels natural, poetic." The real triumph of Levete's pavilion is this fusing together of the natural and the technological. This is a very human space, in its scale and delicacy, it doesn't feel cold like it has been simply printed from a computer.

The key to achieving this effect lies in the process of making. "We really wanted to explore the limits of a material," Levete says, "to create something impossibly fragile, but which has a strength to it." From the start, she knew this wouldn't be something that a regular builder would be capable of. Through an introduction from the engineers, Arup, Levete approached ShapeShift Design Technologies, a composites company in Brisbane with a history of making high-performance racing yachts. "We showed them our sketches and discussed over the phone what we wanted to do," Levete says, "and they just immediately embraced the idea and were challenged by it. We were extremely lucky to find the right partners first time off."

In many of Levete's projects this pushing at the edges of design and construction often demands collaboration with experts beyond architecture. What is arguably one of Levete's best known projects—the Media Centre at Lord's Cricket Ground in London, created in 1999 with her late partner Jan Kaplicky—was also famously made by boat builders. But where Lord's exploited the boat builders for their ability to create non-uniform shapes at a large scale—like those of a boat's hull—the MPavilion exploits this expertise at a smaller scale, for its material capacity.

The design for the MPavilion 2015 was driven by a process of experimentation and trial and error, a constant to-and-fro between the fabricators and the architects, seeking to achieve this vision of a fragile structure, swaying in the wind. "It was far more complex to achieve than we'd imagined," says Levete, who describes the particular challenges of working with materials that sound more like ingredients for a Heston Blumenthal dessert than off-the-shelf architectural components. In order to create the translucent petals out of resin, they required some support structure. Too much structure, and the petals would feel heavy and contained, losing their delicacy. Too little structure, and they would just flop about with no integrity.

With the fabricators, a solution was found to enclose carbon and fibreglass strands between two layers of resin, threaded together to form a delicate pattern. The team had to work double shifts to add the next layer of resin at just the right moment, before the other had set too much. "It was fantastic to work with people who were really interested to explore the limits," says Levete. The columns, also made of carbon fibre, were sourced from Finland, where they were made to serve as camera tripod legs. Being hollow, the columns allowed the necessary bits of wiring for lighting and sound to be concealed inside. Working with lighting designer Ben Cobham of bluebottle, the MPavilion project management team and composer Matthias Schack-Arnott of Speak Percussion, an audiovisual artwork was commissioned by the Naomi Milgrom Foundation. This was performed each evening of the 2015 program season. The sound of six resonant gongs was synchronised with the LED lighting to form an 'evening ritual', marking the transition from day to night in this 'digital forest'.

The result is something delightful and unexpected. On visiting the pavilion, my first instinct is to lie down on my back to gaze up at the woven roof of overlapping petals. I lift my legs up, leaning them against one of the carbon fibre columns. The black stitching in the petals is not unlike the black stitching of my Nike Flyknit shoes. This is architecture in tension, light and athletic, ready to sprint away, not heavy and grounded, here to dominate you with its mass.

This distinction between light and heavy architecture recalls one of the great philosophical arguments of the nineteenth century, when two accounts of the origins of architecture fought it out head to head. In one corner, stood the French architect Marc-Antoine Laugier, who argued that architecture has its fundamental origins in the column: "Its perfect verticality gives it its greatest strength." This lineage began with the so-called 'Primitive Hut', a rough-hewn shelter of bare timber, and reached its epitome with the stone temples of ancient Greece and Rome. Laugier argued that all architecture should therefore aspire to solidity and mass, which in his time meant rejecting the delicacy of the Baroque, in favour of the bombast of the Neo-Classical.

In the other corner stood the German architect and theorist Gottfried Semper, who argued instead that architecture has its origins in four elements: the hearth, the roof, the mound, and—most notably—the enclosure. Unlike Laugier's heavy walls, Semper's enclosure was made of woven textiles, stretched between lightweight timber frames, such as those he learned of in the vernacular architecture of the Caribbean.

But what does this centuries-old debate on the origins of architecture have to do with today? Well, perhaps with the exception of some airport roofs, we all live in Laugier's world. The vast majority of buildings are made of compressive material, whether concrete, brick or steel. Few architects aspire to the lightness of Semper's 'enclosures', remaining content simply to pile up bricks. Levete's pavilion instead reaches back to recover this unrealised trajectory of architecture, creating a building that is delicate and taut, springing, rather than heaving. It is a part of nature, a part of the park, evoking the feeling of sheltering under a tree, as well as being a finely-wrought piece of architectural technology.

"One of our preoccupations is to always test the limits of things," says Levete. It is for this reason that invitations to experiment, such as the MPavilion commission, are so critical to the development of architectural ideas. Weaving together nature, place, technology and architectural history, Levete's MPavilion can show us both where we have come from, and where we are going next.

Dr Rory Hyde is the curator of contemporary architecture and urbanism at the V&A Museum, design advocate for the Mayor of London, and adjunct senior research fellow at the University of Melbourne.

MPavilion 2015 by Amanda Levete of A_LA was gifted by the Naomi Milgrom Foundation to the people of Victoria and relocated to Dockland Park on Collins Street, Melbourne in 2016.

p. 72–73
Photography: Richard Powers.
p. 74–83
Photography: Rory Gardiner.

DESIGN PROCESS

2014–2019

85

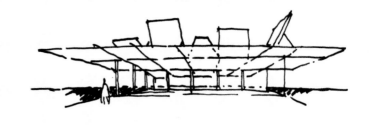

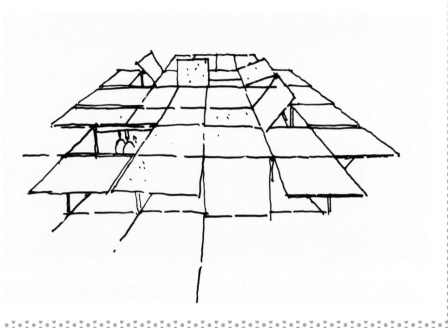

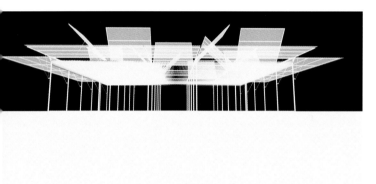

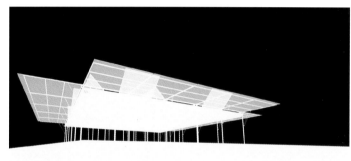

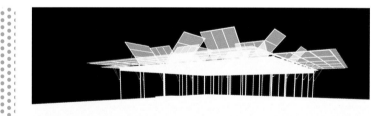

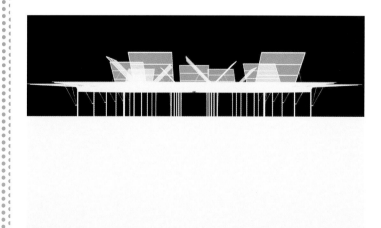

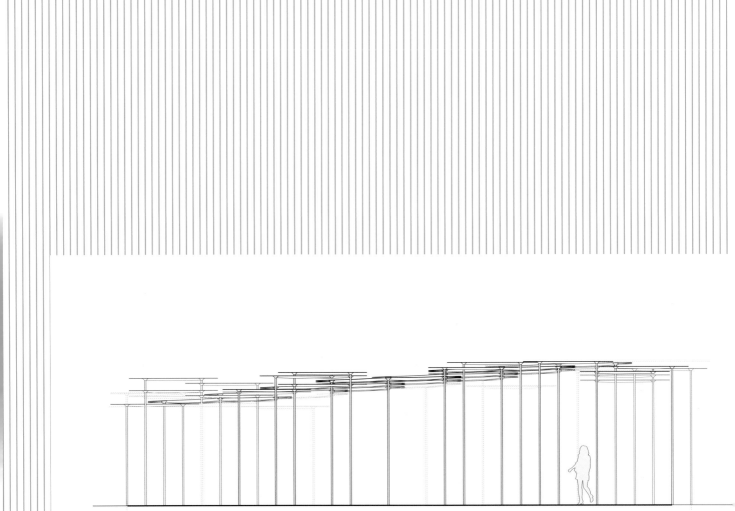

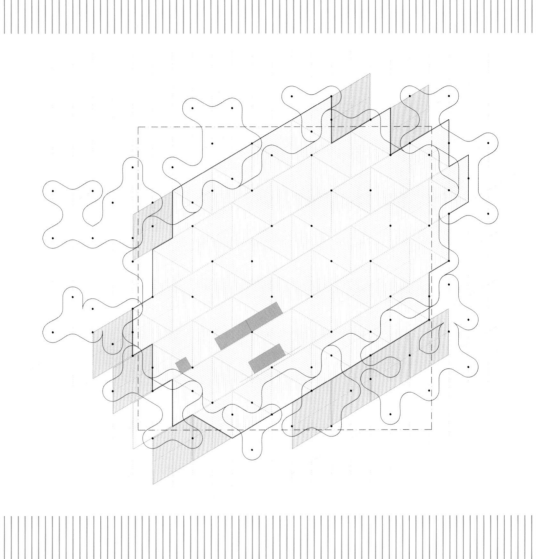

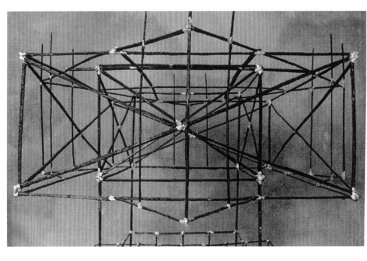

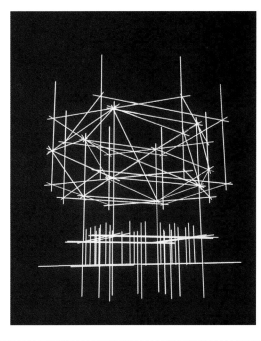

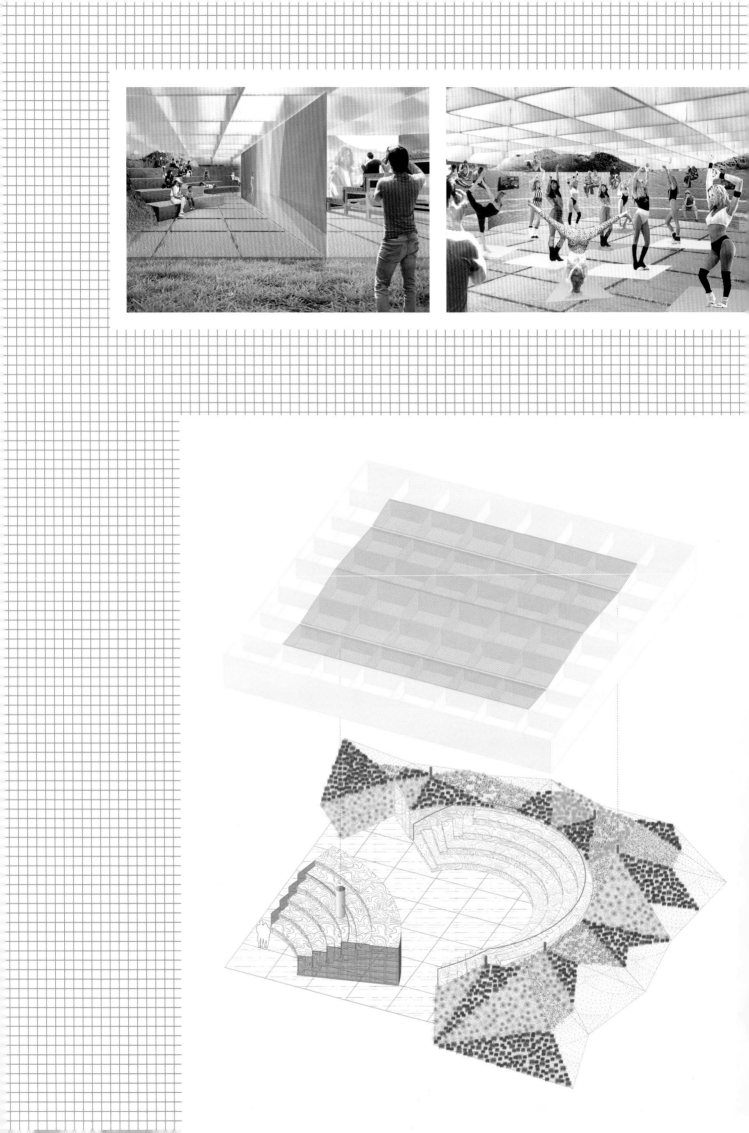

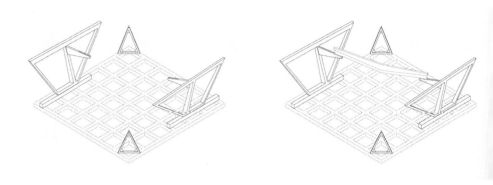

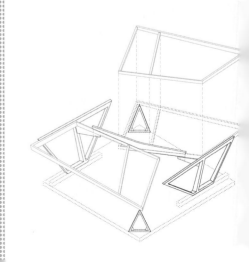

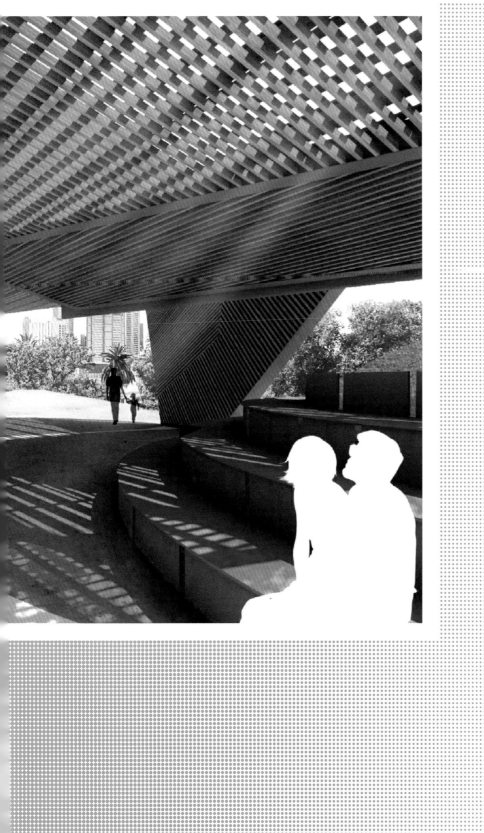
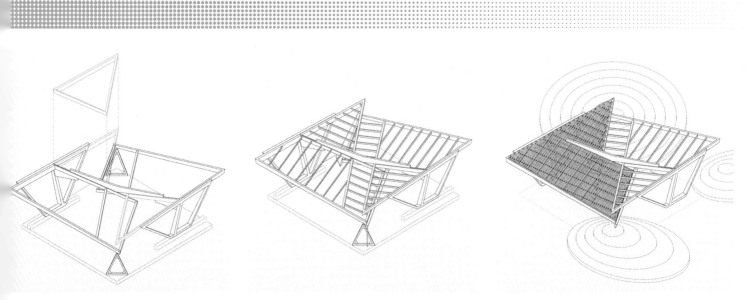

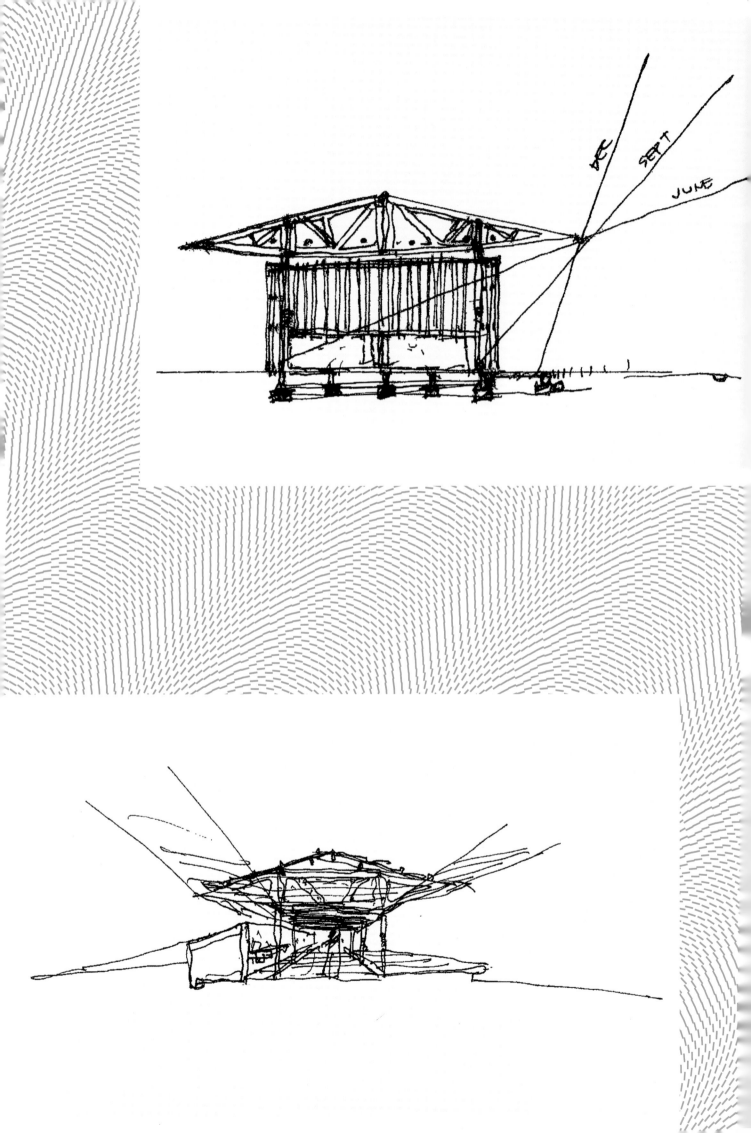

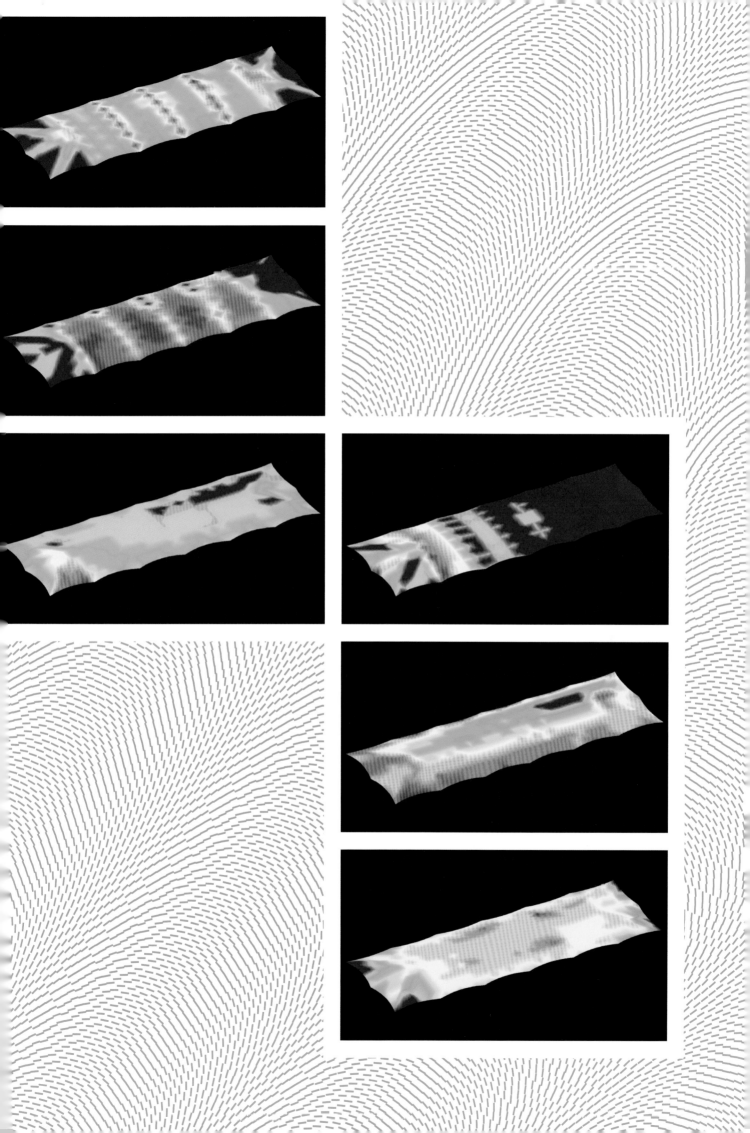

p. 86–87
MPavilion 2014 renders and sketches
by Sean Godsell Architects.
p. 88–89
MPavilion 2015 renders and drawings
by AL_A.
p. 90–93
MPavilion 2016 sketches by Bijoy Jain
and models by Studio Mumbai.
Photography by Nicholas Watt.
p. 94–95
MPavilion 2017 renders, drawings and
model by OMA.
p. 96–97
MPavilion 2018 renders and drawings
by Estudio Carme Pinós.
p. 98–99
MPavilion 2019 sketches by Glenn Murcutt
and renders by Pattons.

BIJOY JAIN
STUDIO MUMBAI

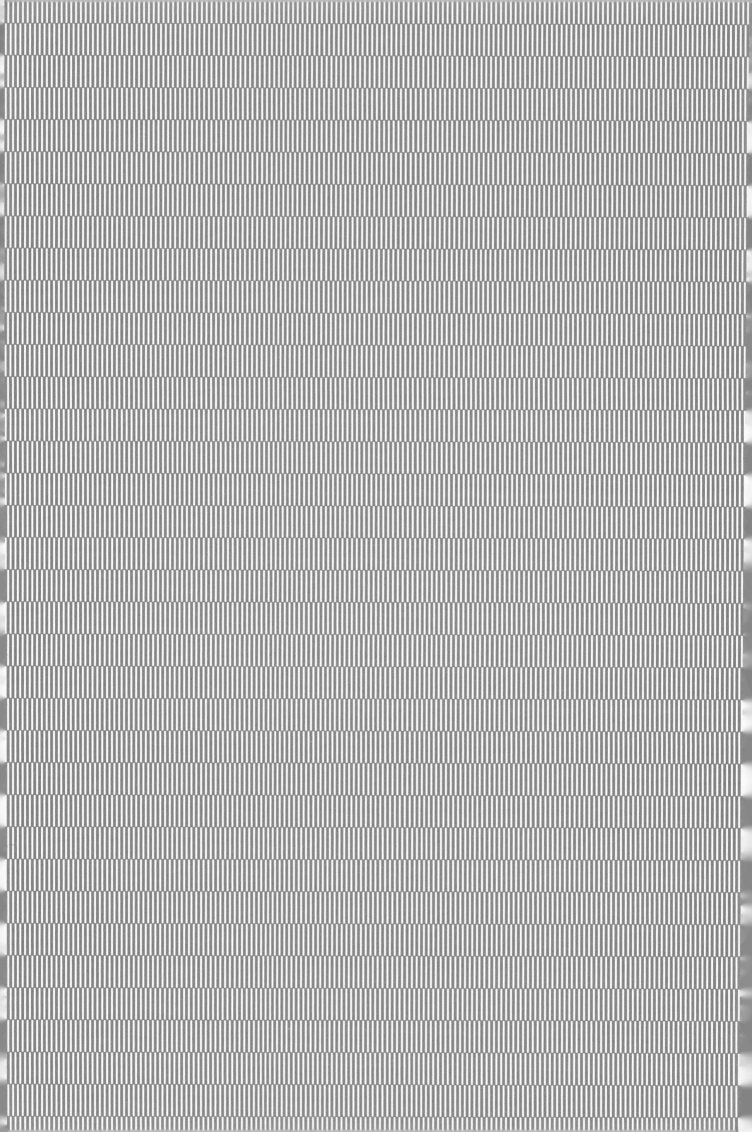

ALL HANDS ON THE PRESENT
ARIC CHEN

There was something jarring about seeing the 2016 MPavilion, designed by the Indian architect Bijoy Jain, in Melbourne's Queen Victoria Gardens. Set among the park's neatly manicured lawns, sprinkled with ornamental palms and British imperial monuments, the woven canopy of Jain's bamboo shelter struck a disjointed silhouette against the city's glass high rises and the imposing 1960s bluestone façade of the nearby National Gallery of Victoria. Appearing out of place and out of time, Jain's MPavilion claimed a surreal, nonlinear presence on the landscape.

The contrast between the pavilion and its backdrop was all the more remarkable given the importance of context to Jain and his work. Best known for his studied engagement with craft, workmanship and materials, Jain creates spaces of quiet elegance whose visceral qualities embody his particular view of architecture as an intertwinement of design, craft, site, materiality, and the experience and activation of space. In the houses, workspaces and installations he designs, courtyards create ambiguous intersections between interior and exterior. Bamboo is juxtaposed with brick, while panels of translucent marble filter light onto walls slathered in earth, cow dung and lime. To visit his studio in Mumbai, with its pigment and fibre samples, rattan-weaving workers, full-scale mock-ups and intricate models—detailed down to the individual bricks—is to get a sense of the milieu in which Jain operates.

Roughly square in plan, Jain's MPavilion is a low-slung bamboo structure with woven karvi awnings arcing gently above Australian bluestone pavement. That its 2016 location, surrounded by modern Melbourne, was in a park built on reclaimed swampland and named for Britain's nineteenth century monarch obscures its former landscape and history. The original owners on the land on which the Queen Victoria Gardens were built are the Yaluk-ut Weelam, part of the Boon Wurrung language group of the Kulin Nation. Prior to being displaced by European settlers in the early nineteenth century, the Indigenous people used this area as a hunting ground and often gathered with other clans nearby. For Jain, this history as a water resource served as a starting point and was invoked by a cylindrical well that he bored into the ground.

"I've always been very curious about what creates a settlement and what provokes us to inhabit the places we inhabit," Jain says. "In this particular case, there was this whole historical palimpsest—what was an Aboriginal settlement, with a source of water, and the layers and layers that became sedimented on top as Australia evolved. It was clear from the beginning I wanted to connect back to the source and anchor it."

Placed slightly off-centre, the well stood beneath a square oculus in the pavilion's roof—made concave, "like when you clasp your hands to hold water," Jain says, so that it funnelled rainwater down below. The structure was like "a big hut to protect that water source," the architect adds, but it was also a means of articulating the relationship between ground, water and sky, noting again the connection Indigenous cultures have to nature, but also that "this connection is a concern that's universal."

At the start of public events in Australia it is now customary to include an Acknowledgement of Country, which recognises that the land on which the proceedings are taking place has Indigenous custodians who did not assent to their displacement from it. Jain's pavilion is rooted on an absence made present. However, his evocation of the site's Aboriginal forebears stops there; it was a reference to which he sought to connect meanings and practices that translate across time and geographies—"an evolution of a communication or a conversation from which an architecture can be produced," he says.

In fact, the MPavilion's roof panels and bamboo were sent from India before being assembled onsite. A freestanding tazia—an architectural construction traditionally used in Indian religious processions—marked the pavilion's entrance. "For me, what was interesting about the tazia is that from region to region, it's always manifested as an architectural object, normally mimicking some kind of building in that region," Jain says. "It's always changing, and here, it became like a totem."

As an Indian architect trained in the United States, Jain wears his own identity lightly, as if it is, in itself, present by virtue of omission. That he works in India, with Indian craftspeople drawing from Indian traditions, seems both integral and incidental at the same time. For all the tactility he brings to architecture, Jain has a tendency to describe his work as existing in the realm of the intangible. He often speaks of the materiality of sound—of "making things with the sound of your breath"—while "the ethos [of a project] is what defines the aesthetic, what drives the form," he says. "The architecture is an incident, simply a reason for it to exist where it exists."

Perhaps seminal for Jain in this regard was his 2010 installation, called 'In-between Architecture', for the Cast Court of the V&A Museum in London. Amid the vast hall's nineteenth century plaster copies of Michelangelo's David and Trajan's Column, assembled in the Age of Empire, Jain inserted a full-scale cast that he had made of an informal dwelling that a family in Mumbai had carved out from a tightly crammed leftover space between a warehouse and his then studio.

The installation literally concretised an inversion of positive and negative space, making visible a void into which marginalised groups often recede. At the same time, like his MPavilion, Jain's intervention in a context highly charged with the legacy of British colonialism couldn't help but be seen in terms of displacement, except in this case the power structures at work were less clear cut.

Jain is uncomfortable with 'absolutes' and the dogmatisms they inspire. Meanings, spaces, and the meanings of spaces, shift constantly. To ask Jain why the well and oculus of his MPavilion were placed off-centre is to have him question why the centre of a space should be understood only in Euclidean terms. There is something refreshingly contrarian, even defiant, about this. For Jain, the somewhat alien nature of his MPavilion was a riposte to the expectations set by the built environment around it. "Who would imagine this structure in Melbourne, in the garden, with the museum, the high rises?" he asks. "I wanted to make a counterpoint to say that this is not in the past; it's present."

Perhaps it's a stretch, but one could argue that Jain's MPavilion is, in fact, highly contextual in a city that, to a casual observer, appears architecturally defined by clashing chronologies. More than most, Melbourne's urban landscape draws into high relief a condensed agglomeration of architectural styles. A single block might yield late Victorian buildings, ingrained with their own eclecticism, alongside variants of brutalism, postmodernism, and seemingly the full array of twentieth century architectural positions—often assertively expressed, and frequently built after they fell out of favour in other parts of the world. Within this lively pastiche where one might find, say, a replica of Oscar Niemeyer's 1943 Capela Curial de São Francisco de Assis cheekily propped atop a 1995 housing estate tower, it is perhaps only natural to discover a tiki hut (as some described Jain's MPavilion) in its midst.

Locality and other pragmatic concerns also left an impact on the structure. The tazia was placed adjacent the main pavilion because its originally intended position, atop the oculus, posed design and structural issues that couldn't be satisfactorily resolved. Humidity prevented the use of the mixture of soil and cow dung that Jain proposed for coating the canopy. Other practical constraints nixed plans to construct the pavilion with locally gathered materials. Building codes, and a local unfamiliarity with Jain's construction materials and techniques, had to be negotiated.

The architect takes a characteristically sanguine view, emphasising the collaborative nature of the pavilion. The project was "really a technological transfer, and a cultural communication, between one place and another," Jain says. Indeed, the construction process saw both the Australian builder, led by Tony Isaacson of Kane Construction (working with the engineering firm Arup), and Jain's studio crisscrossing between Melbourne and Mumbai to learn about, test and oversee the various building elements. What's more, the pavilion required not only kilometres of rope to bind its bamboo poles together—but also the assistance of a scout troop and dozens of architecture students, working on weekends, to do the binding. "I wanted to, in some ways, not be rigid about the aesthetic of this thing; it was more of a framework for interaction, which came from the people involved in making it," he says. "It inhabited an in-between space, somewhere between complete and incomplete. But the spirit remains."

It should come as no surprise then that the MPavilion's opening marked a different sort of culmination for Jain. On that evening, the architect watched the inauguration ceremonies as the Yorta Yorta soprano and composer Deborah Cheetham AO performed a song she had written for the occasion. And as she took to the stage, "that was a very powerful moment for me, the moment the pavilion came alive," Jain says. "In some ways, it became complete, as if the space was invited to occupy the land."

Aric Chen is curator at large for the M+ Museum for visual culture in Hong Kong, and professor of practice at the College of Design & Innovation at Tongji University in Shanghai.

MPavilion 2016 by Bijoy Jain of Studio Mumbai was gifted by the Naomi Milgrom Foundation to the people of Victoria and relocated to the Melbourne Zoo in Parkville in 2017. The building has since been modified.

119

p. 106–117
Photography: Rory Gardiner.
p. 118–119
Photography: Courtesy MPavilion.

MPAVILION 2017

REM KOOLHAAS & DAVID GIANOTTEN

OMA

THEATRICS, SPECTACLE AND THE CITY
ELLIE STATHAKI

It could be argued that the smaller a design project is, the more challenging it becomes. What large-scale work demands in architectural mastery through its sheer size and complexity, a small project makes up for with its unyielding need for precision and brevity. In a mixed-use complex, the challenges stemming from scale and activity may seem obvious and anticipated; yet it is the small-scale projects that can become real brain teasers, incorporating a range of needs in a fairly succinct physical presence.

Pavilions fall firmly in the latter category; and MPavilion—arguably one of the most high profile examples of its kind—is no less of an architectural riddle. The project's ambitious brief outlines a compact structure that allows for several readings; an innovative public space for all to use freely; a design-led 'object' that promotes great architecture to a wider audience; and an actual and symbolic platform for live cultural debate.

Usually relatively small, and often temporary, pavilions are almost always public and somewhat open-ended in terms of their use. There are park follies, bandstands, fun outdoor seating structures and sun-shading canopies—but more often than not, pavilions are a place where life alfresco unfolds, often in unexpected ways. "It's an open situation, we never know how the public will use it, and it's free and here for everyone," Hans-Ulrich Obrist said recently of the Serpentine Pavilion at the opening of the 2019 structure, designed by Junya Ishigami.

On one hand, a lack of a strict formal and functional definition can be a blessing when it comes to design, offering the architect ample creative freedom for experimentation. In fact, not only can usual rules and restrictions appear looser in this type of commission—often seen as a cross between a building and an art piece—but the design must actually make a point of being fluid enough from inception, in order to accommodate a host of activities, scheduled and spontaneous. The result is small yet perfectly formed; a volume that seems simple, but there's clearly more than meets the eye here. The MPavilion series' structures are conceptually and visually powerful, as well as potentially physically complex—and quite fittingly so, for a space conceived to become a multi-layered stage for Melbourne's urban life and ongoing architectural discussion.

At the same time, a pavilion's open-endedness invariably comes hand in hand with openness, in the literal sense. Pavilions are outdoors creatures—as well as social ones. So when Rem Koolhaas and David Gianotten at Office for Metropolitan Architecture (OMA) were called upon to design the 2017 MPavilion in Melbourne, they turned their attention towards past examples of open-air structures. In particular, ones that played a key role in their communities, such as those found in the largely outdoors-orientated cultures of the Mediterranean. Ancient Greece and Rome offer a wealth of examples and OMA state the historic open-air theatre of Syracuse, Italy (a UNESCO World Heritage site, built by the Greeks in the fifth century BCE) as a key source of inspiration.

Drawing on its influence feels natural, as this typology has since become visible in almost every society and culture, explains Rem Koolhaas, who led the project together with David Gianotten. "An orientation of what has been done before in a particular domain is always key for us. For example here we looked at ancient theatres as well as the tradition of the Serpentine Pavilions, where we actually participated [in 2006]. We try to offer something new, while doing what every pavilion has to do, i.e. to be an inviting and pleasant space that inspires curiosity."

With a simple brief to protect visitors from the elements and use an existing grid-based foundation, OMA's design team turned its attention towards the specific structure's role and context to further hone its design approach. Far from being 'just' an architectural gesture, the MPavilion initiative was always meant as a platform for debate and an enabler of activities. Addressing the structure as a key piece in Melbourne's urban fabric, the architects explore the overall form not as a self-containing piece, but as a part of the city's overall current dynamic.

OMA is well versed in the challenges and opportunities surrounding the Australian urban paradigm. In 2012 they worked on a site-specific masterplan study for Sydney and currently have a number of ongoing projects in the country, such as the Western Australian Museum in Perth, which is scheduled to open in 2020. "So we tried to also have a dialogue about Melbourne and its issues and problems. How do you deal with them? And how can you have some of that debate inside the pavilion?" contemplates Gianotten. "The dialogue was much more than just the pavilion, it was also about the program, about Melbourne and the tension that was in the air about certain topics."

"MPavilion 2017 is a public venue with an intimate scale," the OMA website declares, and therein lies the architect's challenge; how to translate that public and social dimension into an appropriate and meaningful physical form. "Everybody praises Melbourne as this most liveable city, but it has significant issues," says Gianotten. "Not only climate issues, but also the car dependency is higher than even American cities. Is it prepared for the future? Melbourne just becomes bigger and bigger, but doesn't really reinvent itself. Policy changes and accommodating increased migration are key issues when talking about the relevance of the urban model of Melbourne and the way it needs to transform."

Combining all those different strands of thought, OMA's response was conceived as a cross between an ancient agora and a theatre—the former traditionally being the heart of the community's athletic, artistic, spiritual and political life, while the latter offering a cross of entertainment, commentary and information on current and historical events, as well as human nature itself. "It was meant like a forum that could perform like a theatre," says Koolhaas. "That's also why it actually only has two elements; the seating arrangement, which is obviously the forum, and the theatre on top, which has all the technical appliances."

The performative elements in these references and their combination are consistent with the practice's philosophy. OMA has a tradition of infusing its work with the orchestration of performance, going far beyond the demands of a brief and into rigorous explorations of forms and uses that break the boundaries of what is expected. It is a notion OMA has explored in depth throughout different projects. "We always try to design a space in a way that encourages different or unexpected uses rather than prescribing everything. This way the building can stay relevant within the context not only in the moment it's finished but also beyond," Koolhaas explains.

"I think that we are using the word 'performance' very often in opposition to 'form'," adds Gianotten. "Architecture is obsessed with form, and because we are reluctant to share that obsession we emphasise the word performance. And what it actually focuses on, this concern, is the question of what can you do more with the same ingredients than the client expects?"

The Naomi Milgrom Foundation's founder, Naomi Milgrom AO, has often spoken about the personal impact of OMA's work. "In the early 2000s I came across Rem Koolhaas's work when I travelled to New York in search of inspiration for contemporary retailing, and the space that stood out was OMA's Prada store in downtown Soho. It was an extraordinary shift in store design —it created a new level of experience and a theatre for fashion."

More recent and current OMA work includes the Taipei Performing Art Centre and Manchester's iconic Factory, each designed to not only serve as 'wrappers' for performance-related events, but also perform in multiple ways themselves. The Taipei project has three stages and reinvents the idea of an auditorium, as well as addressing the theatre as a public space, while the Factory—an expansive warehouse redesign— strives to become an ultra-flexible venue for the widest range of arts to encourage cross-pollination and new relationships. In comparison, MPavilion may appear minuscule, yet the approach does not differ and its multi-layered significance is by no means lessened by size. Gianotten and Koolhaas worked closely with the Foundation to better define MPavilion's form according to its public program. OMA saw the space as a 'cultural laboratory', and tried to make it more interactive "for people to not only consume it but actually participate in it," says Gianotten.

The wide range of potential activities to be accommodated meant that design adaptability was crucial. The idea of movement was invoked, "and this is typically not done in pavilions," says Koolhaas. MPavilion's physical expression, formally (and conceptually) draws on the open-air theatre, featuring a series of fixed curved steps, embedded into the land and garden around it. A separate, movable, rotating section allows for an ultra-flexible performance area that can be configured in different ways according to the requirements of the event or activity. This means the pavilion can shift positions and roles between audience and stage, performer and guest, blurring boundaries and opening up possibilities for collaboration.

The architects wanted the seating space to feel closer to nature, so the structure sits in a garden made up of twelve different species of plants that are indigenous to that part of the world, enhancing its sense of place and embedding it into its local setting. The roof is a technical grid device, so the material of choice was more industrial: metal. Featuring a pronounced aluminium sheet-clad fascia of some 180cm and lending a strong sense of substance and horizontality to the overall composition, the roof is an element that signals the pavilion's presence in the park with confidence.

OMA's philosophy of approaching MPavilion as a cultural laboratory yielded results. Due to popular demand, the structure's life on the site was extended and the program logged record visitors. High profile guests were part of an imaginatively varied program of events, ranging from architectural discussions to activities revolving around hot and relatable topics, such as new parenthood and placemaking. It comes as no surprise that following its service at Queen Victoria Gardens, OMA's MPavilion found a new home at Monash University's Clayton campus, where it is now permanently located, continuing to play its role as a valuable event and community hub that celebrates architectural innovation.

Ellie Stathaki is architecture editor at *Wallpaper** magazine. A trained architect, she studied architectural history at the Bartlett in London and after a brief time in architecture practice, she focused on architecture journalism.

MPavilion 2017 by Rem Koolhaas and David Gianotten of OMA was gifted by the Naomi Milgrom Foundation to the people of Victoria and relocated to the grounds of Monash University, Clayton campus in 2018.

p. 126–127
Photography: Timothy Burgess.
p. 128–129
Photography: Laurence Bolhaar.
p. 131
Photography: Gavin Green.
p. 132–133
Photography: Rory Gardiner.
p. 134–139
Photography: Timothy Burgess.

ARCHITECTURAL MODELS

2014–2018

141

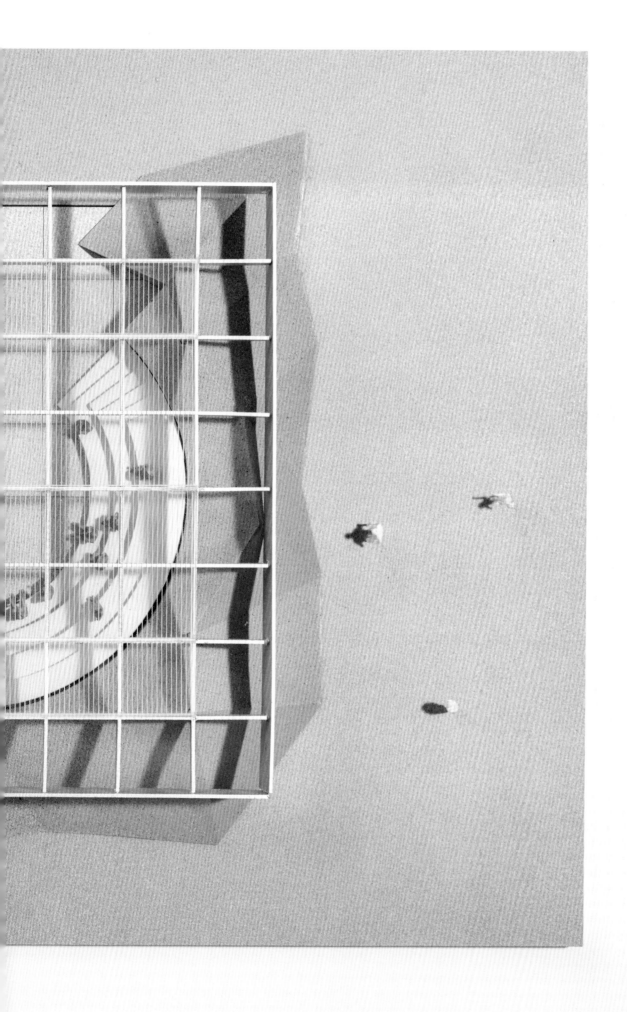

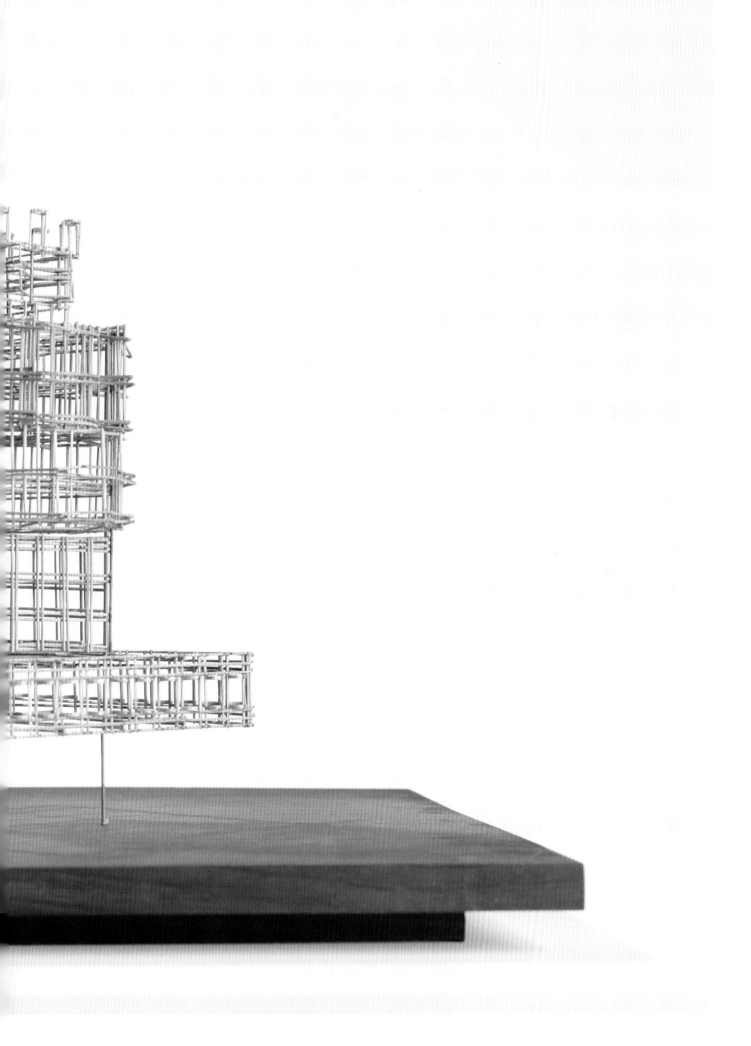

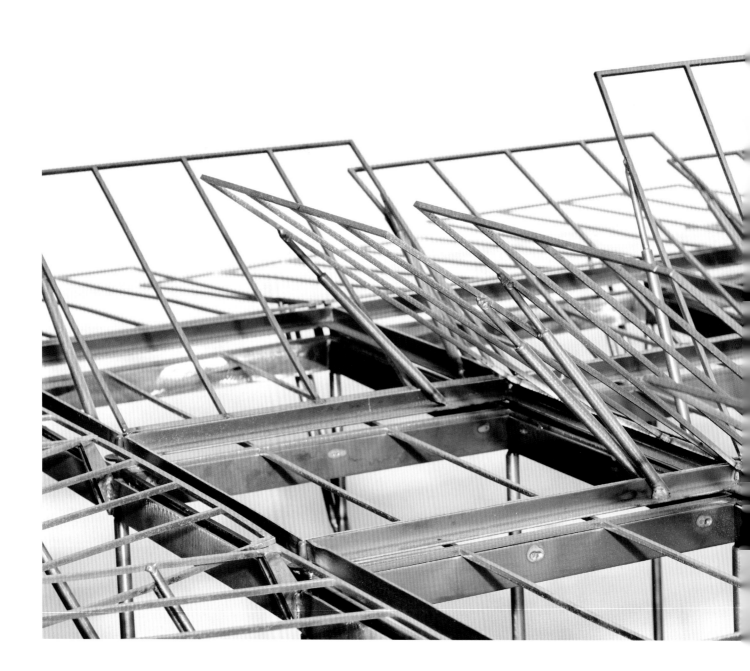

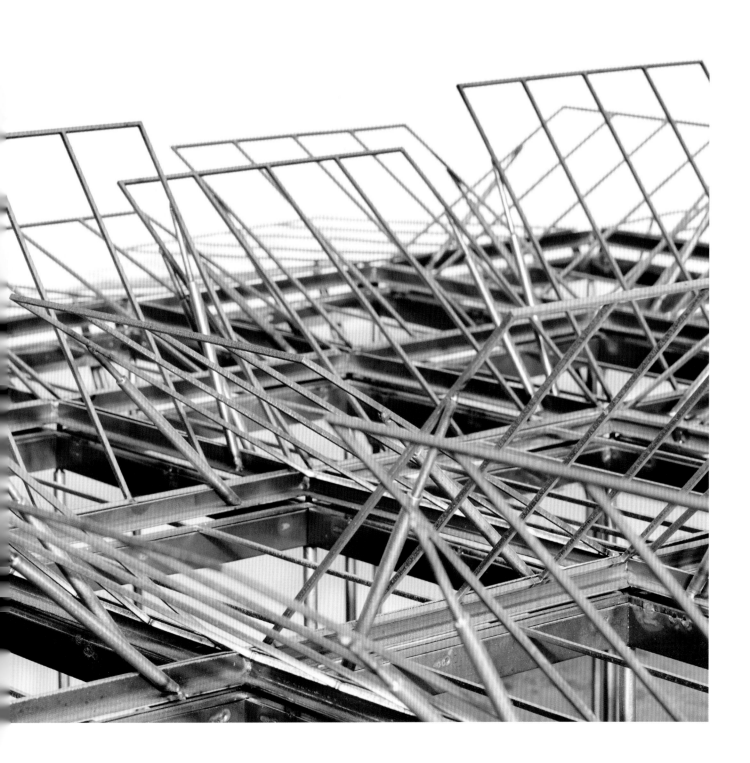

p. 142–143
Model of MPavilion 2017 by OMA.
p. 145
Model of MPavilion 2016 by Studio Mumbai.
p. 146–147
Model of MPavilion 2016 by Studio Mumbai.
p. 148–149
Model of MPavilion 2014 by Dayne Trower,
Sean Godsell Architects.
p. 151
Model of MPavilion 2018 by
Estudio Carme Pinós.

Photography: Tom Ross.

CARME PINÓS

ESTUDIO

CARME PINÓS

A DESIGN FOR EVERYONE
CAROLINE ROUX

"An architectural project is more like making a film than a sculpture," says Carme Pinós, the Catalan architect who designed MPavilion 2018. "First you must write the script, and to do that you have to understand the site, and then how it will work for the people who will use it. Architecture is a catalyst for encounters and relationships, it's about experience."

Pinós says Naomi Milgrom gave her total freedom when commissioning the design, and had only one condition: "She said, 'Design us something that reflects your ideas, but please protect us from the rain'." Pinós herself was drawn to the idea of playing with water. "Well, it was a bit of an obsession, to be honest," she reveals. "I wanted the people inside the pavilion to be able to see the water when it rained, but not be drowned out by the noise, so we made the roof in two layers of timber latticework with polycarbonate in between. The timber controlled the sound while the polycarbonate lent transparency." On rainy days, the pavilion was enhanced by the very elements from which it was protecting visitors. When the sun was out, the lattice work offered a play of shadows and light.

Pinós believes in allowing the architectural language and form to develop according to need. She says she begins each project by identifying what she doesn't want from it. Each project is an adventure in which, at the beginning, I do not know where I am heading, but I know where I do not want to go. I come at the site with questions that arise from the the client's requirements and from what the place wants." Her MPavilion, however, wasn't entirely a *tabula rasa* for the architect. Hers is the fifth in the series, after all, and she had keenly observed how the previous one, by David Gianotten and Rem Koolhaas, had been used. The amphitheatre it contained had been particularly successful, and she would create one in her own. But the concrete floor concerned her. "The first time I went there, it was full of children playing, and I thought they deserved something gentler." The soft rubber surface she chose didn't just offer its younger users more protection from knocks and bruises, but also provided a transitional sensation for all visitors as they crossed into the pavilion, from feeling earth and grass underfoot to something suddenly springier.

Pinós's other consideration was the context: a beautiful park, with a dramatic urban skyline where nature, albeit of a designed variety, prevailed. "As humans, we should strive to be in dialogue with nature and not dominate it," she says. She inserted her pavilion between two mounds, eliding it with the existing landscape, while it also served as a place offering a series of framed views from within. "It really is a very simple structure," she says. "It's like a bent sheet."

Pinós's respect for nature is more than just architectural lip service *de nos jours*. She was born and grew up in Barcelona, but spent long periods of her childhood on a big farm in the north of Catalunya, in a house that she describes as continually under construction and also filled with art. For her, nature and art have always existed in the same place, but a deep engagement with landscape underpins many of her projects, from a summerhouse in Mexico—that's a neat series of horizontal and vertical planes in stone, steel and glass—to hotels in Puerto Vallarta and Majorca where new buildings snake almost invisibly across the delicate sites. "I was the only daughter," she says. "My father decided that one child should be a chemist, one an agronomist and one an architect. So I took that third role. From the age of fourteen I never questioned it."

She started her studies aged seventeen. There were two hundred students on her course, four of them women. Even today, her sex isn't entirely unrelated to her participation in the MPavilion project, part of whose remit is to support diversity in architecture (though gender parity in the profession is gradually becoming a reality, Naomi Milgrom is still keen to foreground the work of women.) Pinós initially worked with her former partner Enric Miralles and the couple completed two now legendary small buildings for the Archery Range of the Barcelona Olympics in 1992. In each building, two architectural languages—the organic and the rectilinear—are wrapped around each other to create an almost deconstructed effect, while in parts perforated walls let in dainty circles of Barcelona sunshine. "It was very beautiful," concedes Pinós, "very risky and completely original." The pair parted in 1991, as soon as it was finished, and Pinós has run her own studio ever since.

The Barcelona Olympics, and the series of three impressive mayors who brought urban renewal to the Catalonian capital, certainly helped to define Pinós's view. "It was a good period for Barcelona. The mayors were interested in creating public spaces and looking at the city as a whole. They didn't give the city to property developers, but took responsibility for how it should grow and change. It wasn't about money, it was about offering the citizen something new and good," she says. "Architecture is a service to society, it changes people's lives and makes society possible. It's a huge responsibility," she continues. "That's why I liked Naomi's MPavilion project—because it's very social, it's for the citizens to use. They can go there and have a coffee, or play their guitar and have an audience. It is not a piece of art."

The pavilion is in tune with Pinós's philosophy on another level, too. "We are past the era of spectacular architecture," she says. "Sometimes we need to find a new language and that time has come. This is the time of free and flexible architecture." The pavilion is little more than a roof, folded like origami, supported on gridded steel columns. To make up for limited internal seating, she also designed flat-pack stools, composed of three pieces of dyed MDF, that can be easily erected or demounted and stored away. "They were made in Barcelona and arrived in our studio in two not-very-big boxes," says Pinós, who took the prototype to Melbourne in her hand luggage, and whipped it out in a meeting, surprising the room with a spot of rapid, dry-jointed assembly.

But bigger buildings, she believes, need to be able to adapt to a variety of roles. "If a project is so specific to its program, if you need to change its function it becomes weak. A church can be a museum—and that is a sustainable position. Now some hospitals, for example, are so specifically made that when procedures change they risk becoming obsolete." Indeed while architecture must have a purpose, for Pinós it will always primarily be grounded in the experience of space.

When Yvonne Farrell and Shelley McNamara curated the Architecture Biennale in Venice in 2018, they declared themselves to be looking for work that "addressed the unspoken wishes of strangers", so it comes as no surprise that they included projects by Carme Pinós in their exhibition. Among them was the Cube 1 Tower in Guadalajara,

Mexico (model now in the collection of New York's MoMA), a seventy-metre-high office building, where three structures cluster around a central void. "It was about creating a building in which all offices are well ventilated, have natural light and take advantage of Guadalajara's good climate. We wanted to eliminate the need for air conditioning," says Pinós. Geometrically complex, though easy enough for the eye to read, the space between these three concrete cores is open to the sky, every office to benefit from double light sources and natural cross-ventilation and the open space at ground level to make the building accessible to passersby.

In Barcelona, when tackling the renovation of the city's historic Boqueria market, and introducing a new art school and housing to an unloved central city square, Pinós spent most time analysing the way the public used the existing space. "If anything defines contemporary architecture in my city," she says, "it is its humanistic quality." The resulting apartments are arranged in a staggered formation, to respect the ragged quality of the original square (really a car park at the back of the market). The art school offers an opaque ceramic façade, to diminish its presence and protect the students' privacy, but inside is like a sky-lit street. As for the market, she extended its roofs to create a pattern of shadows across the square, effectively functioning as a sundial. "I call it urban suture," Pinós says of the solution, which respected the past of one of Barcelona's medieval quarters. "It's about working with and between history and natural phenomena."

Carme Pinós had been on Naomi Milgrom's radar for a while, before she was contacted regarding the MPavilion. "It was a surprise to get the call," says Pinós, who later met Milgrom in London to discuss the commission further. "We started to find some strong common points," says Pinós. "Not least our love of Balenciaga, so we went to see an exhibition of his work at the V&A Museum." Pinós, who had studied pattern cutting in her youth (there was no fashion college in Barcelona, or perhaps she would have chosen a different course) was able to explain the Spanish couturier's very particular sectional cutting system to the Australian visitor. Needless to say this cemented a burgeoning relationship, which has gone from strength to strength.

With MPavilion completed, Pinós has gone on to design another project for Milgrom. "Architecture in itself is not so difficult," says Pinós. "It is a response to a set of conditions and needs. What makes it complicated is the rules, the municipality, the developer, the fact that costs have to be cut and then cut again." In Milgrom, she has found a client who allows her room to grow.

Caroline Roux is a London-based arts writer and regular contributor to the *Financial Times*, the *Observer* and *The Art Newspaper*.

MPavilion 2018 by Carme Pinós of Estudio Carme Pinós has been gifted to the people of Victoria by the Naomi Milgrom Foundation and will be relocated to a permanent site in 2020.

p. 158–161
Photography: John Gollings.
p. 163–169
Photography: Marie-Luise Skibbe.
p. 170–171
Photography: Courtesy MPavilion.

MPAVILION 2019
GLENN MURCUTT

A TABLECLOTH UNDER A WING
FRANÇOISE FROMONOT

Designing a temporary pavilion for a public park in the middle of a major city is a dream project for any architect. Whether the designer is a talent in the making or a seasoned starchitect, such an exceptional commission promises an aesthetic exercise relatively free of the constraints that more conventional programs have to deal with, and can be a rare opportunity to produce a small manifesto. The history of modern architecture abounds with examples of this kind, from the works of the 1920s avant-gardists who were able to take advantage of universal expositions to test their revolutionary architectural concepts, right up to the selection of international architects showcased by the Serpentine Pavilions for close to twenty years in London's Hyde Park. The program Naomi Milgrom has created for her MPavilion appears as a felicitous continuation of this fertile lineage.

When Glenn Murcutt AO was entrusted with the design of MPavilion 2019, the result was bound to be a little bit special. In the five decades of running a solo practice from his tiny Sydney office, Murcutt, in a sense, has never stopped designing pavilion manifestos. He has turned hundreds of small lightweight houses into an exemplary modern typology for Australia and its distinctive landscapes. It is extraordinary that a singular, rigorous practice that has deliberately restricted itself to small-scale projects, exclusively in his own country, has met with such enthusiasm throughout the world, as demonstrated by the many prestigious international prizes Murcutt has been awarded.

The metal structure crowned with a fabric wing-like roof that forms Murcutt's MPavilion can accordingly be read as another key element in a lifetime's work, by an architect who has elevated the pavilion to the status of an ideal, as though in response to the successive etymologies of the term. From the Latin *papilio* (root of the French *papillon*, butterfly), to the Old French *pavillon* (tent) and the English 'pavilion', which adds a stately note (large decorated tent), Murcutt's buildings tap into the cross-cultural origins of this essential model.

These light, refined shelters can touch down everywhere (though not just anywhere), without causing irremediable damage to the land, being sensitive to the place they fit into, and embodying a set of principles that are to their architecture what DNA is to living organisms. Driven by ecological convictions from which he has never deviated, Murcutt has made every one of his projects a statement about the right way to inhabit a territory, even if—as here—no more than temporarily. For him, the personality, aims and ethics of a potential client have always been important criteria in accepting jobs. Persuaded that "for any good project, there is always a good client," Murcutt has often claimed to be wary of working for anonymous institutions. He prefers to have direct personal relations with the people commissioning him, whether a family (with houses), a board of trustees,[1] or representatives of a specific community.[2]

1
Buildings such as the Arthur & Yvonne Boyd Education Centre, Illaroo, designed in collaboration with architects Wendy Lewin and Reg Lark.

2
The Australian Islamic Centre, Newport, designed in collaboration with architect Hakan Elevli.

This personal connection allows him to work with a close understanding of the client's aspirations, and to get a finer grasp of the program's cultural context. Milgrom's invitation to design the 2019 iteration of MPavilion offered Murcutt an opportunity to put his principles to the test through the challenge of producing a small civic space, while further refining them through dialogue with this exceptional client, in a shared desire to contribute to the life of the city.

Even if they appear in deliberate contrast with their settings, Murcutt's buildings are never solitary objects, but relational devices. Their value does not lie first and foremost in how they look, but in the possibilities they open up. The fluid open plan of their common spaces enables a variety of everyday uses, whereas their envelopes contain everything needed to adjust their interior mood to the changing climatic conditions of their environment. At the interface of nature—ground, sky, weather—these light skins negotiate the relationships between human needs and physical contexts. Large adjustable façades open at will on the sheltered side, beneath projecting roof eaves calculated to the millimetre to let in or screen out the sun, depending on the time of day and the seasons. Roofs are adapted to the geography, taking the most appropriate shape to drain away rainwater and deflect prevailing winds. These domestic pavilions are also small 'machines for perceiving' their locations. Carefully placed openings reveal the most remarkable features of the buildings' surrounding landscapes, framing specific vistas, trees or rocks. They also allow occupants to experience the cosmic elements, which the architecture renders palpable. Light—sunlight, and even moonlight—can flood the rooms or filter in through adjustable louvres. Air circulates in a very controlled way across the buildings' thin compartments, through the porous membranes of the façades and the pivoting blades of the blinds. Rain and hail can be felt by their sound, which is broadcast into the interior via thin metal roofs. The inhabitants are both protected from and connected to the cycles of nature, made tangible by the building: transcribing nature into design becomes another way of domesticating it.

Together, these features define the fundamental tenets of an ecological architecture, in the fullest sense of the term, meaning an architecture that is 'appropriate to place', as Murcutt likes to say. His buildings are designed to add to 'System Earth' exactly what we need, but no more, to be able to inhabit it.

With his pavilion-like houses, his larger-scale projects and with his MPavilion in a landscaped park, the siting of a building is always the first, crucial step. The new construction needs to avoid disturbing the underlying logic of the terrain while anticipating the inevitable transformations brought by the activities it will accommodate over the course of time. Murcutt is well versed in tried-and-true design solutions and from his extensive architectural knowledge extracts examples that nurture his own work. Fascinated by biology and botany, he is an astute observer of natural systems and of the forms they generate. He looks at the way trees and plants adapt to habitats, and he extrapolates that rationale to the human realm. Murcutt likes to weave lessons drawn from his experience of various landscapes into his projects, interpreting the behaviours they elicit and turning them into anthropological paradigms. In his work on MPavilion, he says he remembered a trip to the Maya ruins at Yaxchilàn in Mexico, when his small plane landed in an airfield hacked out of the tropical jungle. In that clearing surrounded by a rugged landscape, there was the pleasure of an improvised lunch under the aircraft's wing: "The tablecloth laid out and the shade of the wing defined place, the place of our picnic lunch." Similarly, for Melbourne, he wanted to create "just a place where you could sit in the shade" so that anyone, at any time of the day or night, can enjoy the events the pavilion will shelter under its roof.

Here, Murcutt's quest for achieving optimal environmental comfort—both climatic and social, using very simple means—began with this question: "Where will I put the tablecloth on this site?" Once the right spot was identified, everything followed logically from the intention to reproduce the magic atmosphere of that Mexican picnic, with its combined qualities of protection and openness, "refuge and prospect". MPavilion 2019 is around 270 square metres, with an internal ceiling height similar to that of a house. In its original location, it opened to the north-east over its long main façade, unfolding layered parallel planes: the park grounds, the Yarra River, and beyond, the skyline of the city centre. Its paved floor defines a flexible all-purpose stage. The structure's regular series of columns, partly anchored in existing pad footings, give the volume weft without enclosing it. A roof made of translucent membrane fabric, sewn in one piece, hovers above the interior volume without compressing it. Its deep eaves extend the feeling of security procured by the covering and taper outwardly to give it a sharp, crisp edge against the sky. Inside, the ceiling's pivoting fabric panels, the absence of walls, the adjustable blinds that screen out southerly winds, and the storage alcoves standing at each extremity "just like bookends", define a space. The interior can be furnished as required, thanks to the fifty or so red coloured stools designed by Chris Connell especially for MPavilion.

Every detail, which in the architect's design for MPavilion 2019 is pared back in the extreme, is planned to scale-up this logic, so that the project's economy produces an aesthetic that is Murcutt's own: the mix of strength and slenderness that characterises the structure, which is fully prefabricated to facilitate assembly and future disassembly; the delicacy of the fabric wrapping the wing-like roof trusses and which, when stretched taut over their lowered arches, forms a series of small domes over the roof's exterior. All around, the eaves' sharp profile, obtained by folding a sheet of stainless steel, replaces guttering: in the Japanese manner, rainwater falls directly from the roof to the ground, into a perimetric drain placed inside a trench and concealed under river gravel. LED lighting concealed in the void between the roof and the ceiling make the pavilion glow like a lantern at night. This is "not minimal", Murcutt says, but a "minimum—of material, of effort—to achieve the most: simplicity, the other face of complexity."

The most experimental part of the project involved the use of fabric as covering—a first for Murcutt. Making a continuous seamless surface required some laborious fine-tuning in collaboration with the manufacturer. Engineering work "confirmed and developed the constructive intuition," says Murcutt. Computation helped to adjust the structure to the constraints of tensioning and wind forces; digital representations of various types of stresses produced images that, he notes with excitement, "look like Aboriginal paintings."

Great conceptual sophistication, then, was required to turn this MPavilion into a simple distinctive 'moment' in a stroll around the park, an in-between space that constitutes, for as long as it stands, a possible common place. The pavilion will be relocated in the future so it can pursue its life cycle, in a gamble that its architecture can continue making sense on another site. In this paradoxical world of ours, which is both increasingly unified by globalisation and fragmented by the antagonisms it exacerbates, Murcutt has, once again, raised the flag of a utopia both small and great: the possibility of a discreetly universal architecture.

Translation by Julie Rose. Françoise Fromonot is a Paris-based architect-academic and architecture critic. She is the author of *Glenn Murcutt: Buildings and Projects, 1962–2003* (Thames & Hudson, 2003), which received the book prize of the Académie d'Architecture.

MPavilion 2019 by Glenn Murcutt has been gifted to the people of Victoria by the Naomi Milgrom Foundation and will be relocated to a permanent site in 2021.

p. 179–191
Photography: Rory Gardiner.

A SECOND LIFE

SIMON TERRILL

193

MPAVILION: A SECOND LIFE

A photographic essay exploring the life of the first five pavilions in their permanent locations—as civic spaces, backdrops and containers of activity. Rather than invent or choreograph, my purpose was to highlight the use of these space as they fold themselves into the life of the city. Shot on colour negative film, the images blend architecture and activity into single masses of light, movement and space. I like to think of the method as playing the scene, sensing a way into the architecture that gives over a being-there to the optics of the camera, sideways glances that hold still something fleeting, in motion, barely glimpsed.

Photography: Simon Terrill.

JOHN TATOULIS
CEO, Hellenic Museum
"The MPavilion 2014 gifted to the Hellenic Museum is a beautiful and functional space. It has helped the museum expand its public programming and to share activities with our network of five cultural museums in Melbourne. It is an ideal space for engaging new audiences in conversation around the arts, cultural stewardship, design and architecture."

JAMES MACKENZIE
Chairperson, Development Victoria
"The installation of MPavilion in Melbourne's Docklands became a catalyst for the creation of a new public space on the corner of Collins Street and Harbour Esplanade. With the arrival of MPavilion, Development Victoria landscaped the existing park, installed new seating, an exercise station and technology facilities to make it central to the life of the people living and working in Docklands."

DR JENNY GREY
CEO, Zoos Victoria
"MPavilion 2017 is a beautifully accessible undercover area that has become a distinctive and adaptable gathering place for visitors to Melbourne Zoo. Its design has inspired us to create new public and educational activities and develop new ideas that we hadn't thought of before."

PROF. MARGARET GARDNER AO
Vice Chancellor, Monash University
"Thanks to the generosity of the Naomi Milgrom Foundation, MPavilion at Monash has become an integral part of campus life, and offers a dynamic and transformative experience within the artistic, educational and cultural life of the University. An incubator for creativity and innovation, with a focus on research, sustainability and inclusivity, MPavilion at Monash is a valuable addition to our existing cultural precinct."

CONTAINER OF IDEAS

It was always intended that what goes on in and around each MPavilion should be as significant as the structure itself. Conceived as a community asset as much as an architectural gesture, the creation of a vibrant four-month free event program, and a commitment to creating a lasting design legacy, has been key to the initiative's success and international profile.

While the Naomi Milgrom Foundation has funded the design and construction of each MPavilion and its annual administration, support from federal, state and city governments, philanthropic trusts and corporate sponsors has helped fund much of the activation and programming. The Foundation's success in developing these relationships manifests Naomi Milgrom's belief in the potency of public–private partnerships.

From the beginning, the Foundation worked closely with the City of Melbourne to improve the facilities and access to the previously under-utilised Queen Victoria Gardens. Landscape designer Paul Bangay provided designs for new perennial garden beds and plantings to frame the MPavilion site and the City of Melbourne installed new lighting to improve public safety and access at night.

Programming for the first MPavilion was facilitated by fostering relationships with established design associations and cultural and educational organisations such as the Robin Boyd Foundation, Melbourne Recital Centre, Australian Institute of Architects, RMIT Design Hub and the University of Melbourne—all of which integrated events into the MPavilion program.

The opening of the first MPavilion was presented as part of the Melbourne International Arts Festival and featured a performance by opera singer Deborah Cheetham, who composed a song to welcome the pavilion to Melbourne in the language of the First People. A song cycle of welcome and reconciliation has been sung by Cheetham or an Indigenous children's choir over the past six years.

Sean Godsell's inaugural MPavilion established the idea of a morning and evening 'ritual', taken up in subsequent event seasons. In Godsell's year, the ritual was the choreographed transformation of his closed metal box pavilion: each morning the structure's forty-five perforated aluminium panels, operated by pneumatic arms, would open like a flower accompanied by a specially commissioned soundtrack.

At AL_A's pavilion, the evening was welcomed with a commissioned son et lumière performance. At Jain's pavilion, the day began with visitors applying a sheet of gold leaf to the shelter's bamboo columns. At OMA's amphitheatre, it was stories of the First People of Melbourne by Yaluk-ut Weelam Elder, Parbin-ata Carolyn Briggs. And for Estudio Carme Pinós's pavilion a meditative soundscape started and finished each day.

During each MPavilion's event season, the diverse roster of activities can include anything from contemporary yoga taught by members of the Chunky Move dance company to presentations of student design projects, or architectural debates with local practitioners—even dog photo booths with a professional pet photographer. Lunchtime recitals, morning book readings, afternoon concerts; 'Bug Blitz workshops' have introduced children to the biodiversity of the ponds surrounding the pavilion.

The MPavilion season of events is rich and eclectic, reflecting the spirit of the city itself. At the same time, international speakers and performers reinforce Melbourne's position as a global city. Australian design legends Penelope Seidler and Mary Featherston have given talks at MPavilion, as have Danish urbanist Jan Gehl; British architect Sir David Adjaye; the former curator of the Musée des Arts Décoratifs, Pamela Golbin; MoMA director Glenn Lowry; and the director of Zaha Hadid Architects, Patrik Shumacher. Each has been invited to use MPavilion as a platform to stimulate conversation and exchange ideas.

Design writing has also been encouraged with an MPavilion prize initiated in conjunction with *Art Monthly* magazine, writers in residence programs and the commissioning of a major history of the MPavilion site, *Miracle Swamp: The place of the Queen Victoria Gardens in the urban, horticultural and creative life of Melbourne*, written by Gina Levenspiel and published in 2016.

Each year, MPavilion also commissions a print issue by Melbourne based small footprint online magazine Assemble Papers. The special editions feature articles inspired by the MPavilion architects and the ideas incorporated in their designs.

The Trisha Brown Dance Company, the Australian String Quartet, French choreographer Xavier Le Roy and Indian musician Dr Aneesh Pradhan are among the hundreds of performers who have used MPavilion as a stage to reach a new audience. In fact, since 2014, the programming team has commissioned and collaborated with more than a thousand individual architects, designers, artists, musicians, writers, performers, curators, academics and thinkers.

Unlike most cultural spaces that require extensive lead times for their programming, MPavilion is deliberately agile. Milgrom and her team understand that each building needs to be not only intellectually engaging, but must also be purposefully engaging. Collaborators are encouraged to think how best to use each pavilion's space, to experiment with it, push its boundaries.

Since access is free and seating is casual, audience members often spread out on the surrounding lawn. And of course, the MPavilion Kiosk serves some of the best coffee in town.

In recent years, MPavilion has become a de facto annex of Melbourne's Bakehouse Studios, hosting surprise performances by national and international bands as they prepare for recording sessions and tours. The 'surprise rehearsals' have been a rare opportunity to glimpse inside musicians' creative process.

The annual MPavilion program has evolved as community groups have become increasingly aware of the opportunity of a captivating venue in a park in a central city location. As of 2017, the curated schedule has been augmented by a call for expressions of interest that enables community groups and individuals to approach MPavilion's programming team with ideas about how to occupy the space. This has allowed the Community Hubs organisation—which serves as a gateway for immigrant families to connect—to bring in parents and children from twenty-four outlying areas on an early literacy program that culminated in a multicultural community picnic. Multicultural Arts Victoria created the 'Our Place, Our Home' event in collaboration with the Melbourne International Arts Festival, celebrating the diversity of people making music across the state of Victoria, with performers revelling in their Congolese, Oromo and Cuban musical roots.

"When the MPavilion was still a new project, we needed to show people the unique opportunity the program presented," says Sam Redston, executive director of the Naomi Milgrom Foundation's MPavilion and Living Cities Forum initiatives. "But with the fourth iteration in 2017 we arrived at a watershed. Community groups and other organisations began approaching us with ideas."

Within its six years of existence, MPavilion has come to be seen as something of a cultural laboratory in the park. It continues its mission to be a free, highly accessible catalyst to promote and foster activity in the design and architecture sectors and the fields of dance, music, visual arts and wellbeing. But it has also extended this foundational raison d'être to use its significant presence and nexus of connections to create a space for the citizens of Melbourne to call their own.

Design workshops and talks include MPavilion's own BLAKItecture forum series, which brings together Indigenous built environment practitioners with the aim of centralising Indigenous voices in conversations about architecture and the future of our built environments.

It was this interest in the future of urban planning that led to the establishment of the Living Cities Forum in 2017. For the past three years, this mid-year design conference has been organised by the Naomi Milgrom Foundation as an international symposium. It features leading architects and urban thinkers from around the world discussing issues of importance to cities and civic spaces. In 2019 it expanded to include forums in Melbourne and Sydney in association with the country's leading architecture and design schools.

Architectural honeypots, the MPavilions draw visitors from across Australia—and serve to further animate Melbourne's Southbank arts precinct. This precinct will soon be further consolidated as the Victorian Government prepares to activate a $1 billion masterplan to create an elevated park, gardens and pedestrian zones, south of the Yarra River to improve the precinct's vital role in Melbourne's culture and economy.

"And it seems that the MPavilions have acted as something of a catalyst for those changes," says Sir Nicholas Serota, Chair of Arts Council of England and a previous speaker at the MPavilion. "The presence within that area of a place that is open, a place that anyone can come to, a place where debate occurs about the future of the city and about the role of new building and of government, architects and developers, seems to have stimulated conversations. The pavilions have become a driver of change."

When the MPavilion project finally comes to a close it will leave a legacy beyond just the relocated structures distributed around Melbourne. It will have kick-started conversations and collaborations with the power to resonate around the world for years to come.

PUBLIC ENCOUNTERS

BOOK READING
THE AUSTRALIAN UGLINESS
LUNCHTIME READING
07.10.2014 – 01.02.2015

Melbourne architect and writer Robin Boyd wrote in his controversial 1960 work *The Australian Ugliness* (F.W Chesthire, 1960), "The basis of the Australian ugliness is an unwillingness to be committed on the level of ideas." A fierce critique of the 'featurism' inherent in Australian suburban architecture, the book was labelled unpatriotic when it was first published, but went on to fuel nationwide debate about design, architecture and urban planning. Each day of the MPavilion 2014 season, guests from local design and arts practices and beyond read from Boyd's influential book—day by day, fifteen minutes at a time, sparking new and healthy debate.

PERFORMANCE →
MELBOURNE FESTIVAL PRESENTS
TRISHA BROWN EARLY WORKS
24.10.2014

Trisha Brown Dance Company—the highly influential American contemporary dance company—visited Australia as part of the 2014 Melbourne Festival to perform sixteen of the choreographer's revolutionary pieces. A program of Trisha Brown's early pieces—including *Group Primary Accumulation*, *Sticks I & II* and *Curl Curve Back Up*— was performed at MPavilion and offered a bite-sized taste of the legendary choreographer's work.

INSTALLATION, PERFORMANCE ↙
SLOW ART COLLECTIVE LEAF HOUSE
MUSIC INSTALLATION
02.11.2014 – 07.11.2014

Slow Art Collective is an interdisciplinary artistic collective established in 2009 by Dylan Martorell, Chaco Kato and Tony Adams. In 2014 it was commissioned to create a large-scale installation for MPavilion that drew on ideas of environmental sustainability, material ethics, DIY culture and collaboration. Over the course of a week, the collective combined bamboo, rope, string, musical instruments and gathered plant debris from MPavilion's parkland setting to create an evolving installation, turning the pavilion into a living studio soundtracked by sonic lullabies.

INSTALLATION, PERFORMANCE →
THE TELEPATHY PROJECT'S STAR
PAVILION
17.11.2014 – 18.11.2014

Australian-based artists Sean Peoples and Veronica Kent were commissioned to create a celestial event as part of Melbourne Music Week at MPavilion 2014. The evenings showcased a mind-widening sonic experience, titled *Star Pavilion*, featuring multidisciplinary performer Sophia Brous. Ufologists, astrophysicists, sci-fi buffs, moonrise howling choirs, Greek gods, sunset dancers and astrologers descended upon the gardens for a dusk-'til-dawn celebration of starry nights and all things celestial.

CHILDRENS' WORKSHOP →
POLYGLOT THEATRE PAPER PLANET
WORKSHOPS
06.02.2015 – 11.02.2015

Polyglot Theatre was commission by MPavilion
to create an interactive and experimental
theatre experience for children and families as
part of the summer school holiday program.
It presented a week-long series of art-making
workshops that transformed MPavilion into
a paper and cardboard jungle. *Paper Planet*
invited participants to jump in—or watch and
enjoy—as the pavilion evolved into a world
filled with tall, wondrous cardboard trees,
paper leaves, scrunched boulders and delicate,
folded creatures, inspiring young minds to
design and create their own urban playground.

PRESENTATION ↘
ALPHA60 X
29.01.2015

Melbourne-based fashion label Alpha60
designed the wardrobe for MPavilion's staff in
2014 and staged a fashion event to celebrate
the label's tenth anniversary. Collaborating with
Snuff Puppets theatre group, the event made
MPavilion the stage for a fashion show watched
from the surrounding gardens—a wonderfully
weird spectacle that also unveiled Alpha60's
Winter '15 collection.

PERFORMANCE
SUNSET RITUAL
05.10.2015 – 07.02.2016

Melbourne-based percussionist Matthias
Schack-Arnott of contemporary music
group Speak Percussion was commissioned
by MPavilion to create a soundscape that
synchronised with an evening lighting display
designed by architect Amanda Levete and
bluebottle lighting designer Ben Cobham.
Gloamer, a six-channel work for resonant
metallic percussion instruments and sine
tones, was based on a detailed analysis of
the overtone structures of thirty-two gongs
and cymbals. The composition ran for twenty
minutes during each night at sunset.

DISCUSSION ↓
PARLOUR PRESENTS WOMEN
TRANSFORMING THE CITY
15.10.2015

An advocacy organisation dedicated to
expanding the spaces for women in Australian
architecture, Parlour led a discussion about the
history of women shaping the Australian city—
its buildings, spaces, and social and political
agendas. At *Women Transforming the City*,
architectural historian Dr Karen Burns, editor
and researcher Justine Clark, social historian
Renate Howe, urbanist Jane Jose and architect
Shelley Penn explored the powerful roles
women have played as activists, architects,
planners, philanthropists, policy makers,
politicians and writers.

MRELAY: HABITAT, RITUAL, TRANSFORMATION AND UTOPIA
30.01.2015

MRelay was devised by Natalie King for MPavilion in 2014 and has been a regular event each year. In a sports relay, a team covers a distance in turns—a baton passing from one runner to the next. MRelay is an intellectual team sport bringing together leading thinkers, philosophers, fashionistas, mavericks, activists, provocateurs, architects and doyennes to share insights and ideas throughout a marathon conversation relay. In 2016, MRelay contemplated our relationship to our natural environments, to our living habits, to change and cultural ideals.

PRESENTATION ↑
MADA PRESENTS WEARING THE INTERIOR CITY
12.11.2015

The next generation of Melbourne architects and designers converged on MPavilion to unveil some unique wearable creations by Monash Art Design & Architecture students. Translating notable Melbourne interiors into costume—including interiors of the Melbourne Recital Centre, Arts Centre Melbourne and ACCA—the students presented their bold architectural costumes, experimenting with pleats, drapes, stitches and folds.

TALK, PERFORMANCE, WORKSHOP
XAVIER LE ROY IN DIALOGUE
28.11.2015 – 12.12.2015

Acclaimed French choreographer, dancer and performance artist Xavier Le Roy worked with MPavilion and the Melbourne contemporary dance association Dancehouse to present a series of talks, performances and workshops with the local dance community over three weeks. With work previously presented in New York's Museum of Modern Art, the Centre Pompidou in Paris, and at Panorama Brazil, Xavier explored the ways in which dance and performance have come to inhabit the public realm, and questioned the commodification of performance by facilitating and discussing collective experience.

TALK, WORKSHOP ↓
NEW BRITISH INVENTORS: OLUWASEYI SOSANYA AND PAUL STOLLER
22.01.2016

The British Council—the UK's international organisation for cultural relations and educational opportunities—supported the Australian visit of two British designers recognised for their innovative approach to design in 2016. Inventor Oluwaseyi Sosanya, developer of a loom specially designed for weaving in three dimensions, and Paul Stoller, managing director of London-founded Atelier Ten's Australian office, spoke at events at MPavilion over the first week of February and ran workshops with architecture and design students.

PERFORMANCE ↓
AUSTRALIAN CHAMBER ORCHESTRA
QUARTET EVENING PERFORMANCE
03.02.2016

As the late-summer sun set on a Wednesday at
the beginning of February, the ACO quartet—
led by Richard Tognetti, the ACO's lead
violinist and artistic director—played its way
through a program of beautiful classical music,
its staccatos and crescendos filling MPavilion's
canopy and flowing out into the surrounding
gardens. Visitors sat back under the stars and
were mesmerised by four members of one of
the world's most lauded chamber ensembles.

INSTALLATION, PERFORMANCE ↘
LIQUID ARCHITECTURE PRESENTS
ENDLESS BUMMER: NEW GEAR
NEW YOU
07.02.2016

Endless Bummer was a new music event
created by contemporary music organisation
Liquid Architecture and commissioned by
MPavilion. Performing inside AL_A's pavilion
and, at times, from the middle of the crowd,
David Chesworth, Makeda and Mino Peric,
took the steering wheel of a new kind of party,
a take on the classic 1966 surf movie *Endless
Summer*. Liquid Architecture also presented
performance art and sound installations at
MPavilion, bringing together a number of local
artists to collaborate during the season.

OFFSITE EXHIBITION →
STUDIO MUMBAI: MAKING MPAVILION
09.09.2016 – 22.10.2016

An exhibition at RMIT Gallery explored the
inspirations and processes of making and
designing MPavilion 2016. It featured models,
material samples, books, photographs, sketches,
videos—all of which have contributed, in
big-and-small but equally important ways, to
the creation of MPavilion 2016. In addition to
samples of materials and modelling sourced
from Studio Mumbai, the exhibition included
photography from Australian photographer
Nicholas Watt.

PERFORMANCE ↑
CLASSICAL INDIAN MUSIC BY ANEESH
PRADHAN
08.10.2016

During the opening weekend of Bijoy Jain's
MPavilion, leading Indian tabla player
Dr Aneesh Pradhan filled the Queen Victoria
Gardens with his renowned percussive rhythms.
Aneesh was accompanied by Dr Adrian McNeil,
a fellow master of the sarod, a twenty-five-
stringed plucked lute, as well as Sudhir Nayak,
a highly acclaimed harmonium player from
Mumbai.

"ARCHITEC CATALYST FO AND RELATIO ABOUT EX

CARME PINÓS

TURE IS A
ENCOUNTERS
NSHIPS—IT'S
ERIENCE."

PERFORMANCE ↑
TRANSPOSITION: A PERFORMANCE
BY ISHARA PUPPET THEATRE TRUST
14.10.2016 – 15.10.2016

Founded in 1986 by Dadi Pudumjee, the Ishara
Puppet Theatre Trust is one of India's leading
contemporary puppet theatres, committed
to creating awareness of the traditions and
techniques of puppetry in India and the world.
A performance of storytelling that depicted
the illusions of love, dealing with the duality
of illusion and reality, the Trust's *Transposition*
encircled MPavilion in colour and drama. This
performance was part of the Confluence:
Festival of India in Australia.

CHILDRENS' WORKSHOP ↓
BUG BLITZ: A BIODIVERSITY
WORKSHOP FOR KIDS
15.10.2016 – 05.11.2016

Bug Blitz is an internationally generated
initiative from scientific, educational and
creative minds to stimulate an active interest
in biodiversity. It is an imaginative, instructive
and rewarding program that brings new
learning and enjoyment of our environment
to people of all ages—especially the enquiring
younger minds. At MPavilion 2016—and in
each subsequent MPavilion season—the Bug
Blitz team led kids on expeditions through
the Queen Victoria Gardens, discovering
the ecosystems of living things that might
otherwise be overlooked.

PERFORMANCE ↓
MELBOURNE SYMPHONY ORCHESTRA
11.12.2016

As part of MPavilion 2016's summer theme
'Architecture in the City', musicians from
the MSO gave three performances—one at
each of the two previous MPavilions at their
permanent locations and a finale concert under
the intricate roof of Bijoy Jain's pavilion. The
musicians performed chamber music for string
quartet including music for dancing by Johann
Strauss and Astor Piazolla and Iain Grandage's
After Silence, an Australian work featuring
birdsong, suitably surrounded by the Queen
Victoria Gardens.

INSTALLATION, PERFORMANCE ↗
LIQUID ARCHITECTURE PRESENTS
CAITLIN FRANZMANN: TREE-TELLING
18.01.2017 – 24.01.2017

In *Tree-telling*, artist Caitlin Franzmann
was commissioned to deploy handcrafted
divination cards as the trigger for experimental
one-on-one encounters between the artist
and MPavilion visitors. The seven cards were
paired with seven sound compositions, each
corresponding to a tree in the Queen Victoria
Gardens surrounding the MPavilion: Canary
Island Palm, River Red Gum, London Plane,
Algerian Oak, Jacaranda, Atlas Cedar and
Lilly Pilly. Selecting a card from the deck,
visitors embarked on a journey that proceeded
from card reading, to a shared walk from
MPavilion to their chosen tree and back, to an
experimental listening session.

INSTALLATION →
HYPNAPOD: SUSPENDED
CARDIOPHONIC SNOOZE PODS BY
THE UNCONSCIOUS COLLECTIVE
09.02.2017 – 14.02.2017

Established by David Patman and Michelle
Boyde as an informal collaboration of
artists, the Unconscious Collective was
commissioned to take over MPavilion for
a week-long experimental and interactive
artwork. Visitors were invited to relax in a
hanging 'Hypnapod'—a suspended, knitted
cocoon designed by Unconscious Collective in
collaboration with Jenny Underwood at RMIT
University's School of Fashion and Textiles. The
soft, hanging pods were equipped with sensors
and speakers that amplified the inhabitants'
heartbeats in real-time. Together, the pods
produced a unique soundscape, which evolved
as heartbeats went in and out of sync.

PANEL DISCUSSION ↓
A TALE OF THREE CITIES: JAN GEHL
IN CONVERSATION
10.02.2017

Leading Danish architect, urban designer and
writer Jan Gehl was joined by Rob Adams
AM, director of city design at the City of
Melbourne, and Monica Barone, CEO at City
of Sydney, to discuss planning cities for people.
The three esteemed guests focused on the ways
in which the cities of Copenhagen, Melbourne
and Sydney had addressed the task in very
different ways.

TALK, OFFSITE
REGIONAL WORKSHOP
03.10.2017 – 06.02.2018

In keeping with Rem Koolhaas's interest
in the idea of the 'countryside', the fourth
MPavilion season saw the initiation of its
regional outreach programming. This included:
talks by Rem Koolhaas and David Gianotten
from OMA on the topic; a number of musical
showcases by artists from beyond urban
borders taking place, with the assistance of
Multicultural Arts Victoria; and Sydney-based
artist Keg de Souza, travelling to Shepparton
to create an alternative map of the area
based on local knowledge and discussing her
experience inside OMA's pavilion. Keg also
appeared at a special offsite MTalks event in
Shepparton, to share the outcomes of her time
spent with local communities on Yorta Yorta
land as part of the project.

PERFORMANCE ↙
PHILIP BROPHY'S STADIUM: A NEO-
TOKYO TERRASOUND COSMOPHONY
06.10.2017 – 11.02.2018

Each day of the MPavilion 2017 season
closed with a twilight ritual, a recorded
composition commissioned by artist Philip
Brophy wafting through the gardens. *Stadium:
A Neo-Tokyo Terrasound Cosmophony* was
created in collaboration with lighting designers
bluebottle for MPavilion, and was a surround-
sound interpretation of one of the key musical
themes from the soundtrack to Otomo
Katsuhiro's 1988 anime film, *Akira*. Philip
performed the composition live on 6 October
to launch the ritual.

INSTALLATION, PERFORMANCE ←
MATTHEW BIRD: AN IMMERSIVE ENCOUNTER WITH THE AFTERLIFE
08.12.2017 – 21.12.2017

Commissioned by MPavilion, artist and experimental architect Matthew Bird created an interactive installation, inviting audiences to experience an immersive and performative encounter with the afterlife. Multidimensional in nature, the installation was realised with the assistance of students from Monash Art Design & Architecture, and during its two-week lifespan at MPavilion welcomed playful public manipulation. The installation culminated in a series of commissioned performances in collaboration with composer Daniel Von Jenatsch, choreographic artist Phillip Adams and fashion designer Pia Interlandi.

INSTALLATION ↙
SWINGS BY OMA
23.12.2017 – 05.01.2018

In the spirit of their MPavilion, which took its cues from archetypal amphitheatres as meeting places for debate and entertainment, OMA's *Swings* installation drew from historical example to both re-contextualise and reinvigorate the simple joy of swings. Deriving inspiration from ancient artefact, contemporary mainstays and nostalgic examples from cinema and popular culture, *Swings* by OMA harnessed movement, irreverence and a sense of play to activate the pavilion as a locus for multisensorial experiences.

INSTALLATION
SOFT BAROQUE: FOAMY FEELING
15.01.2018 – 21.01.2018

With *Foamy Feeling*, Soft Baroque—aka the London-based contemporary design duo Saša Štucin and Nicholas Gardner—were commissioned to create a site-specific furniture installation. Inflated by polyurethane foam, the soft entities served the comfort of the audience and became both inanimate spectator and participating performance member in the pavilion. A series of air-tight membranes were filled with soft polyurethane expanding foam and slumped over the MPavilion's stairs before being cured, triggering unusual and unexpected sculptural forms.

WELLNESS WORKSHOP
CHUNKY MOVE CONTEMPORARY YOGA
30.01.2018 – 06.02.2018

Acclaimed Australian contemporary dance company Chunky Move constantly seeks to redefine what is or what can be contemporary dance in an ever-evolving Australian culture. So it is that Chunky Move came to lead morning yoga workshops at MPavilion 2017, engaging its experienced teachers and focusing on balancing the energy of body and mind to gain strength, flexibility and balance. The sessions were hugely popular.

FORUM
BLAKITECTURE
15.10.2018 – 21.01.2019

MPavilion's second annual BLAKitecture forum brought together Indigenous built environment practitioners on the Yaluk-ut Weelam land of the Boon Wurrung people with the aim of centralising Indigenous voices in conversations about architecture, the representation of histories, the present state and the future of our built environments. In 2018, the series presented five discussions, ranging from considerations of how Indigenous built knowledge can be taught, to the role of design in memorialising Indigenous history. The forum was curated by MPavilion's program consultant Sarah Lynn Rees.

WORKSHOP, PERFORMANCE ↗
SENSILAB PRESENTS BIG EARTH
LISTENING
15.10.2018 – 03.02.2019

MPavilion teamed with Monash University's SensiLab for one of the biggest MProjects undertakings of the 2018 season. Part science experiment, part art project, *Big Earth Listening* turned the sounds of the earth around MPavilion into an immersive listening and virtual reality experience. Using special microphones buried under and around the pavilion, the work uncovered sounds from inside the earth, turning insects and traffic rumblings into an evolving composition able to be heard on the SensiLab website. The project culminated in a live performance.

PERFORMANCE
MULTICULTURAL ARTS VICTORIA
PRESENTS OUR PLACE, OUR HOME AND
STATE OF CULTURE
21.10.2018

Multicultural Arts Victoria's *Our Place, Our Home* event celebrated the extraordinary range of people making music in Victoria today, with performers tapping musical energies from Congolese, Oromo and Cuban cultures. The event sprang from MAV's *State of Culture* music program, which for more than a decade has uncovered the most dynamic and diverse artists in Australia and propelled them into the spotlight.

DISCUSSION, WORKSHOP
FIXPERTS COMMUNITY ENGAGEMENT
DESIGN INTERVENTION
07.11.2018 – 20.12.2018

A creative and social campaign that utilises design to help people with everyday problems, Fixperts launched in the UK in 2012 and subsequently engaged universities and communities in more than eighteen countries. In conjunction with RMIT's School of Design, MPavilion welcomed the first Fixperts project to be conducted in Australia, facilitating and hosting a six-week program that paired design students with community members requiring vital design solutions. The outcomes were lifelong and exponential, from an enhanced motorised scooter that offered better mobility to students and community members further engaging in social campaigns and professional development.

CELEBRATION ↓
ONE YEAR OF YES CELEBRATION
17.11.2018

To celebrate the one-year anniversary of
Australia saying 'Yes!' to marriage equality,
MPavilion staged an event unlike any in
its history. Three couples and their family
and friends gathered for three very special
weddings in the gardens. The joyous events
were followed by a picnic open to the whole
community, with radio station JOY 94.9
broadcasting live and My Best Friend's
Wedding DJs providing the soundtrack to a
whole lot of love.

FAMILY EVENT
COMMUNITY HUBS FAMILY PICNIC
13.01.2019

Serving as a gateway to connect families with
each other, with schools and with existing
services, Community Hubs Australia reflects
MPavilion 2018 architect Carme Pinós's
interest in creating community cohesion
and nurturing inclusivity. Recognised as a
leading model to engage and support migrant
women with young children, the organisation
works with dozens of communities under the
national program. At MPavilion, Community
Hubs Australia reached out to diverse groups
in Victoria and led parents and children in an
early literacy program, also bringing families
together for an open community picnic.

PRESENTATION ↓
RMIT MASTER OF FASHION (DESIGN)
GRADUATE SHOWCASE
14.11.2019

Part of MPavilion 2019's opening night
celebrations, RMIT University presented its
stunning annual showcase of work by graduates
of the School of Fashion and Textiles Master
of Fashion (Design) program. This was the fifth
presentation of RMIT's graduating masters
students at MPavilion.

PERFORMANCE →
MELBOURNE MUSIC WEEK PRESENTS
SOUND BATH
15.11.2019

A journey into sound and the senses, this
morning event as part of Melbourne Music
Week invited visitors to relax in the tranquil
surrounds of MPavilion and submit themselves
to a restorative ritual of ambient sound,
performed live by gong practitioner Mona
Ruijs, collaborating with Rory McPike of Rings
Around Saturn.

PERFORMANCE ↓
DEBORAH CHEETHAM & DHUNGALA
CHILDREN'S CHOIR PERFORM CHORAL
CONNECTION SONG BOOK
14.11.2019 – 16.11.2019

Deborah Cheetham was first commissioned
to perform at the opening of MPavilion 2014
and her involvement as singer, composer
and conductor has become a six-year
tradition. The 2014 commission was the first
contemporary composition in the language
of the Boon Wurrung and these ongoing
contemporary compositions in the original
languages are an important act of reconciliation
that create a shared understanding of our past
and a way of going into the future together.
At the event on 16 November, the Dhungala
Children's Choir lead by Deborah Cheetham
in conductors role—showed why they are the
peak choral performance group for Indigenous
children in Victoria. The group performed
songs from the *Choral Connection Song Book*,
written by Deborah Cheetham to enable the
children to reconnect with and celebrate their
Indigenous language.

ACTIVITY ↙
DOG WALKING ADVENTURES IN THE
CITY WITH TOM + CAPTAIN
14.11.2018 – 22.03.2019

MPavilion's favourite human–canine duo
returned in 2019 to lead a dog-filled meander
through the city's laneways, arcades and streets,
beginning in the Queen Victoria Gardens.
As usual, the event was enormously popular,
bringing pups and their people out to enjoy a
stroll and prove that the city is a place for all
walks of life.

PANEL DISCUSSION
AIA, AILA AND PIA PRESENT
INDIGENOUS CULTURAL INCLUSION:
HOW ARE WE ENGAGING?
22.11.2019

In May 2019, Ken Wyatt became the first
Indigenous Australian to hold the role of
Minister for Indigenous Affairs, and the first to
sit in Cabinet. Since 2018, several Australian
universities have also created new leadership
roles for Indigenous advisers. This has coincided
with the development of major new works that
embed Indigenous cultures, knowledge and
practices in campus development. This panel
session focused on emergent thinking and work
across a broad range of contexts, with a focus
on where we might and must go in future.

PERFORMANCE
MELBOURNE MUSIC WEEK PRESENTS
COMMUNAL SOURCE
22.11.2019

An immersive experience as part of Melbourne
Music Week, this event presented by South
of the City and Stargazed Records brought
together music, dance, performance and
visual art in an effort to overwhelm the senses
and ask the question: What is the intangible
source of joy that art brings? Inside MPavilion,
musicians created a cacophony and visual
artists projected their creations; dancers moved
to the rhythm of the music, and performance
artists administered semi-ritualistic practices.

PUBLIC ENCOUNTERS

Photography: Courtesy MPavilion.

COMMISSIONS

2014–2019

221

MPAVILION VISUAL IDENTITY
2014–2019
Studio Ongarato has been responsible for
MPavilion's visual identity and print material
since its establishment in 2014. Each year the
identity is changed to reflect the character
of the architects' design and the idea of
MPavilion as a 'container of ideas'.
Design: Studio Ongarato.

MPAVILION 2019 STACKING STOOL
AND BENCH
To honour MPavilion 2019's architect and
Australia's only Pritzker Architecture Prize
laureate Glenn Murcutt AO, the Naomi
Milgrom Foundation commissioned a stool
and bench for MPavilion 2019 to celebrate the
architect's 50th year in architectural practice.
Design: Chris Connell, Chris Connell Design.
Manufacturer: grazia&co., Melbourne.
Material: Powder-coated metal tube frame,
       square metal grid mesh wrap.
Dimensions: 450D × 470W × 460H;
       450D × 2000W × 460H

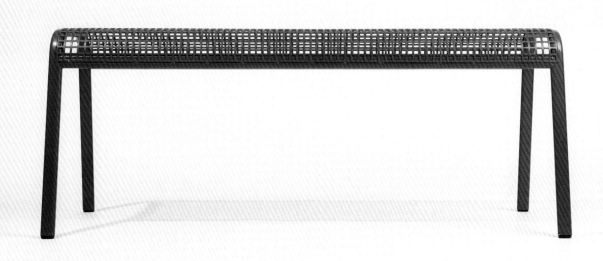

MPAVILION 2017 BADGE
A series of Rem Koolhaas quotes inspired by
OMA themes were reproduced on badges worn
by MPavilion 2017 staff.
Design: Studio Ongarato.

MPAVILION 2017 STOOL
Design: OMA.
Manufacturer: European Ceramics, Perth,
Western Australia.
Material: FLORIM CEDIT Matrice
    porcelain slab.
Dimensions: 400D × 400W × 400H

MPAVILION 2014 TOTE
The MPavilion 2014 tote was made from the
recycled vinyl billboard wrap that surrounded
the building site.
Manufacturer: Locally made in Melbourne.
Material: Recycled vinyl.

MPAVILION 2019
UNIFORM AND BELT
The team at The Social Studio worked closely
with the MPavilion team to design the boiler
suit. The Social Studio, a non-for-profit,
improve the lives of young Australians who
come from a refugee or migrant background
using the vehicle of a fashion business—
including a clothing label, retail shop, clothing
manufacturer and digital printing studio to
create social change. Beloved Melbourne
designer-illustrator, Beci Orpin collaborated
with MPavilion to create a colourful and
functional utility belt.

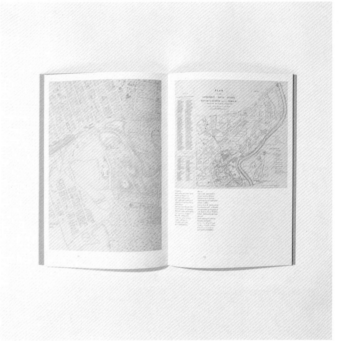

MIRACLE SWAMP BOOK
*Miracle Swamp: The Place of Queen Victoria
Gardens in the urban, horticultural and
creative life of Melbourne* was a publication
commissioned by the Naomi Milgrom
Foundation and supported by Gordon
Darling Foundation. The book is the first
comprehensive history of the Queen Victoria
Gardens in Melbourne and documents how
it became the site of the MPavilion project.
Author: Gina Levenspiel.
Design: Stuart Geddes.
Publisher: Naomi Milgrom Foundation, 2016.

MPAVILION 2017 T-SHIRT
The MPavilion 2017 t-shirt incorporated
a series of OMA renders.
Design: Studio Ongarato.
Material: Cotton

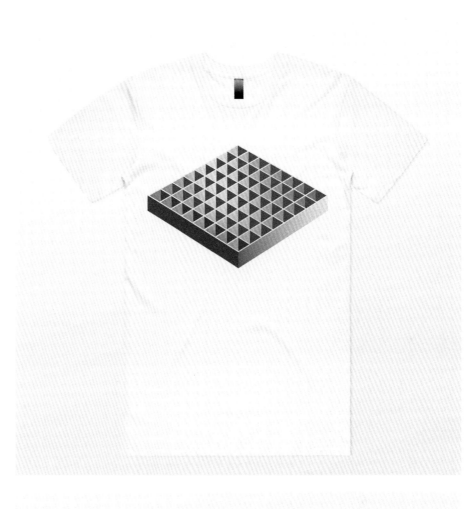

MPAVILION 2014
CHAIR AND STOOL
Commissioned chair and matching stool
designed for the inaugural MPavilion and
sponsored by Laminex Australia.
Design: Sean Godsell, Sean Godsell Architects.
Manufacturer: Workspace Commercial
Furniture, Adelaide.
Material: Steel, laminex solid surface.
Dimensions: 440D × 420W × 720H

MPAVILION 2018 VEST
The vest designed by Melbourne based artist
Esther Stewart was developed as a utility
style garment for the MPavilion staff. Inspired
by cycling and fishing vests, the garment is both
practical and a place to store useful objects.
Design: Esther Stewart.
Manufacturer: Hannah McMullin.
Material: Canvas and neon trim.

MPAVILION 2016 SHIRT
Inspired by cross-cultural references Mischa
Hollenbach and Shauna Toohey of the P.A.M
fashion label, created a one-off print for the
MPavilion 2016 shirt.
Design: Perks and Mini (P.A.M.)
Manufacturer: Perks and Mini (P.A.M.)
Material: Cotton.

MPAVILION 2018 STOOL
The stool commissioned for MPavilion for
2018 is comprised of three pieces assembled by
intersection, making them perfect for a space
used in multiple ways. The stool was designed
to store flat, and can easily be disassembled.
Design: Carme Pinós, Estudio Carme Pinós.
Manufacturer: Focus Taller –
    Francesc Rubio, Spain.
Material: Birch plywood.
Dimensions: 380D × 550W × 440H

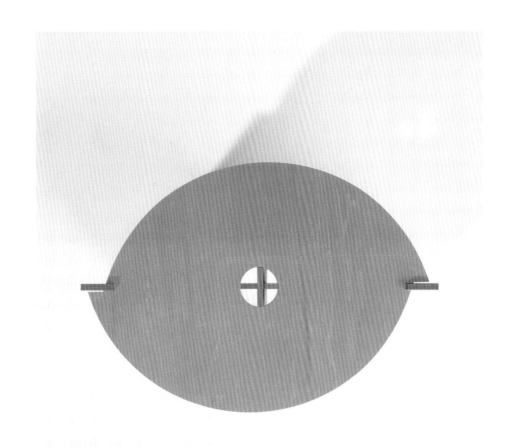

MPAVILION 2016 STOOL
A stool representing the handmade techniques
of local artisans in India was customised by
Bijoy Jain for MPavilion 2016.
Manufacturer: Craftspeople in Mumbai, India.
Material: Locally sourced timber.
Dimensions: 310D × 310W × 530H

Photography: Tom Ross.

COLLABORATORS

ORGANISATIONS

A–Space
2017–2019

Aphids
2018

Art Monthly Australasia
2015–2016

Arts Centre Melbourne
2014–2019

Assemble Papers
2014–2019

Australia India Institute
2015–2016

Australian Centre for Contemporary Art
(ACCA)
2016–2019

Australian Centre for the Moving Image (ACMI)
2014–2016

Australian Institute of Architects (AIA)
2014, 2017–2019

Australian National Academy of Music (ANAM)
2014, 2016, 2018–2019

Australian String Quartet (ASO)
2016–2017

Australian Youth Orchestra (AYO)
2014–2019

Bakehouse Studios
2017–2019

Bedroom Suck Records
2015–2016, 2018

Bug Blitz Trust
2016–2017, 2019

Celia Fox
2015–2016

Ceres
2019

Chunky Move
2017–2019

City of Melbourne
2014–2019

Community Hubs Australia
2018–2019

Dancehouse
2015

Design Institute of Australia (DIA)
2017–2019

Dhungala Children's Choir
2014–2019

Happy Melon
2015–2019

Honey Fingers
2015–2019

Hope St Radio
2018–2019

Hugh D T Williamson Foundation
2014–2019

Hyphen Labs
2018

Indigenous Architecture and Design Victoria
2015, 2017–2018

La Trobe University
2016–2018

Liquid Architecture
2014–2019

Melbourne Design Week
2019

Melbourne International Arts Festival
2014–2019

Melbourne Recital Centre
2014–2019

Melbourne Symphony Orchestra (MSO)
2014, 2016, 2019

Melbourne Theatre Company (MTC)
2018–2019

Monash University
MADA Faculty of Art, Design & Architecture,
SensiLab, MADA Gallery and MUMA
(Monash University Museum of Art)
2014–2019

Multicultural Arts Victoria (MAV)
2017–2019

New Architects Melbourne
2017–2019

Office of the Government Architect
2018–2019

Open House Melbourne
2016–2018

Parlour: Women, equity, architecture
2015–2016, 2018–2019

Planning Institute of Australia
2017–2019

RMIT University
RMIT Design Hub, RMIT Gallery,
School of Architecture and Urban Design,
School of Art, School of Design,
School of Fashion and Textiles
2014–2019

Robin Boyd Foundation
2014–2017

Rock Academy
2018–2019

Royal College of Art (RCA)
School of Architecture
2019

Sibling Architecture
2016–2017

Signal
2014–2019

Soft Baroque
2017

Speak Percussion
2015–2016

State Library Victoria
2016–2019

Swinburne University of Techonlogy
School of Art, Social Sciences and Humanities,
School of Design
2014–2019

The School of Life
2015, 2019

The Social Studio
2019

The Wheeler Centre
2014–2019

Tom & Captain
2015–2019

University of Melbourne
Melbourne School of Design (MSD)
2014–2019

Victorian Premier's Design Awards
2019

Westside Circus
2014, 2017–2019

Yarra Pools
2017–2019

ADELE VARCOE
Fashion activist
2016

ALI BIRD
Media lawyer, producer, curator, *Real Life*
2015, 2017, 2019

ALICE OEHR
Artist, designer
2015–2016, 2019

AMY AND ADAM COOMBES
Fashion designers, *Kloke*
2015 .

AMY MULLINS
Executive director, *Women's Leadership Institute Australia*
2016–2017

ANDREW MCCONNELL
Executive chef, *Cumulus Inc., Cutler & Co. and Supernormal*
2015

ATLANTA EKE
Dancer, choreographer
2014, 2016, 2018

BARRIE BARTON
Co-Founder, *Right Angle Studio*
2014–2015

BECI ORPIN
Artist, designer, illustrator
2015, 2017, 2019

BEN COBHAM
Lighting designer, *bluebottle*
2014–2019

BEN EVANS CBE
Director, *London Design Festival*
2014–2015

BROOK ANDREW
Artist
2014, 2016

CAITLIN FRANZMANN
Artist
2015–2017

CARLO RATTI
Architect, engineer, inventor, educator,
Massachusetts Institute of Technology, MIT Senseable City Lab, 2018

CHEN QIULIN
Artist
2015

CHRIS CONNELL
Furniture designer, *Chris Connell Design*
2019

CHRISTOPHER BOOTS
Industrial designer, *Christopher Boots*
2017–2019

CHRISTOPHER SANDERSON
Co-founder, *The Future Laboratory*
2014, 2016, 2018

CLARE COUSINS
Architect, founder, *Clare Cousins Architects*
2016, 2018

CONRAD STANDISH
DJ
2014–2016

CRAIG JEFFREY
Director, *Australia India Institute*
2015–2016

DAN GOLDING
Academic, writer, *Swinburne University*
2018–2019

DARREN SYLVESTER
Visual artist
2015

DEBORAH CHEETHAM AO
Soprano, composer
2014–2019

DR TARSHA FINNEY
Architectural urbanist, *Royal College of Art*
2019

EMMA TELFER
Director of culture & strategy, *Assemble*
2014, 2016–2019

ESTHER ANATOLITIS
Executive director, *National Association
for the Visual Arts*
2015–2019

ESTHER STEWART
Artist
2018

EUGENIA LIM
Video, performance and installation artist
2015, 2017–2019

FARAH FAROUQUE
Board chair, *The Social Studio*
2019

FLEUR WATSON
Curator, *RMIT Design Hub*
2014, 2016, 2018

GILBERT & GEORGE
Artists
2015

GLENN LOWRY
Director, *Museum of Modern Art (MoMA)*
2014–2015

GRAZIA MATEIRA
Founder, *grazia&co.*
2019

HANS ULRICH OBRIST
Artistic director
2014, 2019

JACK SELF
Architect, director, *Real Foundation*
2017

JANA PERKOVIC
Writer, editor, *Assemble Papers*
2017–2019

JEREMY MCLEOD
Architect, founding director,
Breathe Architecture
2015, 2018–2019

JILL GARNER
Architect, *Office of the Victorian Government
Architect*
2014–2019

KEG DE SOUZA
Artist
2017

KENNY PITTOCK
Artist
2015–2016

KERSTIN THOMPSON
Architect, principal, *Kerstin Thompson
Architects*
2016, 2018

LEAH JING
Writer, photographer, editor, *Liminal Magazine*
2018

LUCY MCRAE
Sci-fi artist, film director
2017

MADDEE CLARK
Writer, Curator
2018–2019

MAMA ALTO
Singer, activist
2014, 2018

MARIE FOULSTON
Videogames curator, *V&A Museum*
2018

MARY FEATHERSTON
Designer
2016, 2019

MATTHEW BIRD
Artist, architect, *Studiobird*
2017, 2019

MATTHIAS SCHACK-ARNOTT
Percussive artist, composer, *Speak Percusssion*
2015–2017

MONA RUIJS
Gong practitioner
2018–2019

NATALIE KING
Curator, editor, professor, *University of Melbourne*
2014–2018

NIC DOWSE
Founder, beekeeper, *Honey Fingers*
2017–2019

OSLO DAVIS
Illustrator
2015

PARBIN-ATA CAROLYN BRIGGS AM
Boon Wurrung senior elder, chairperson,
Boon Wurrung Foundation
2014–2019

PAUL BANGAY
Landscape designer, *Paul Bangay Garden Design*
2014–2019

PAUL GORRIE
Filmmaker, musician, DJ, youth project worker
2019

PENELOPE SEIDLER
Architect, *Harry Seidler & Associates*
2016

PENNY MODRA
Editorial director, *The Good Copy*
2014—2018

PHILLIP ADAMS
Performing artist, artistic director, *BalletLab*
2015, 2017

REBECCA COATES
Director, *Shepparton Art Museum*
2015, 2017–2018

ROB ADAMS AM
Director city design and projects,
City of Melbourne
2014–2019

ROSS HARDING
Creative sustainability consultant,
Finding Infinity
2019

RUEBEN BERG
Architect, founder, *Indigenous Architecture
Design Victoria*
2017, 2019

SARA SAVAGE
Writer, editor, broadcaster, DJ
2016–2019

SARAH LYNN REES
Architect, *Jackson Clements Burrows
Architects*
2017–2019

SHELLEY LASICA
Performing artist
2014, 2016–2017

SIMON WINKLER & LAUREN TAYLOR
Radio hosts, *Triple R*
2019

SIR DAVID ADJAYE OBE RA
Founder, principal architect, *Adjaye Associates*
2016

SIR NICHOLAS SEROTA CH
Art historian, curator, chair, *Arts Council
England*
2018

SIR PETER COOK RA
Founder, architect, lecturer, writer,
Archigram Group
2018

SOPHIA BROUS
Performing artist
2014–2016

SULLIVAN AND SHEENA
DJ duo, *Sullivan and Sheena*
2018

TAI SNAITH
Artist, curator, writer
2014–2017

TIMOTHY MOORE
Architect, director, *Sibling Architecture*
2016–2017

CATHERINE MOSBACH
Founder, landscape architect, *Mosbach Paysagistes*
Living Cities Fourm 2019

CHRISTOPHER HAWTHORNE
Architecture critic, chief design officer, *City of Los Angeles*
Living Cities Fourm 2019

DAN HILL
Director of strategic design, *Vinnova* design advocate for Mayor of London
Living Cities Fourm 2017

DR ADRIAN LAHOUD
Dean, architect, *Royal College of Art (RCA)*
Living Cities Fourm 2019

DR RORY HYDE
Curator, *V&A Museum*
Living Cities Fourm 2017

JANE HALL AND
AUDREY THOMAS-HAYES
Creative collective, *Assemble Studio*
Living Cities Fourm 2018

LIAM YOUNG
Architect, filmmaker, performer, founder, *Tomorrow's Thoughts Today*
2 Living Cities Fourm 2018

MABEL O WILSON
Designer, cultural historian
associate professor, *Columbia University*
Living Cities Fourm 2019

MARISA YIU
Founding partner, director, *ESKYIU*
Living Cities Fourm 2017

MIMI ZEIGER
Critic, editor, curator, instigator
Living Cities Fourm 2017

MINSUK CHO
Founder, architect, *Mass Studies*
Living Cities Fourm 2017

NICHOLAS LOBO BRENNAN
Co-founder, architect, *Apparata Architects*
Living Cities Fourm 2018

RACHAPORN CHOOCHUEY
Co-founder, architect, *all(zone)*
Living Cities Fourm 2019

RYUE NISHIZAWA
Architect, director, co-founder, *Office of Ryue Nishizawa, SANAA*
Living Cities Fourm 2018

SASKIA SASSEN
Sociologist, urban thinker
professor, *Columbia University*
Living Cities Fourm 2018

"EVEN WITH MODEST ART PROJECTS CHANGING "

REM KOOLHAAS

THE MOST
CHITECTURE
YOU ARE
, YOU ARE
HE WORLD."

ACKNOWLEDGEMENTS

FOREWORD
Naomi Milgrom AO

CONTRIBUTORS
Stephen Todd
Dame Julia Peyton-Jones DBE
Dr Rory Hyde
Aric Chen
Ellie Stathaki
Caroline Roux
Françoise Fromonot

EDITORS
Alexandra Zafiriou
Robert Buckingham

PUBLISHER
Kirsten Abbott
Thames & Hudson Australia

DESIGN AND ART DIRECTION
Studio Ongarato

COPY EDITOR
Adam Curley

RESEARCH
Isabella Woolcott

NAOMI MILGROM FOUNDATION
Chair: Dr Kathy Alexander
Directors: Mary Vallentine AO,
    Naomi Milgrom AO
Special advisers: Dame Julia Peyton-
    Jones DBE, Genevieve Timmons
Secretary: Craig Holland

FOUNDING MPAVILION CREATIVE DIRECTOR
Robert Buckingham

MPAVILION TEAM
Current: Sam Redston, Louise Nicholson,
    Alexandra Zafiriou, Jen Zielinska,
    Debbie Prouse, Renee Hoy,
    Isabella Woolcott, Sarah Lynn Rees,
    Paul Douglas, Lauren Squire.
Past: Robert Buckingham, Natalie King,
    Jessie French, Rachel Elliot Jones,
    Charlotte Cornish, Sara Savage,
    Vinisha Mulani, Adam Curley,
    Daniel Gladys, Alan Weedon,
    Etta Curry, Bec Capp.

SPECIAL THANKS
Premier of Victoria Hon. Daniel Andrews MP,
Minister for Creative Industries Hon. Martin
Foley MP, Minister for Priority Precincts
Hon. Gavin Jennings MP, City of Melbourne
Lord Mayor Sally Capp, Parbin-ata Carolyn
Briggs AM, Shayne Elliot, Rob Adams AM,
Sir Nicholas Serota CH, Fabio Ongarato,
Ronnen Goren, John Wilson, Joseph Johnson,
Natalie Boyle, Tony Isaacson, Karen McCartney,
Julia Campbage, Stuart Geddes, Earl Carter,
John Gollings AM, Richard Powers, Rory
Gardiner, Nicholas Watt, Tom Ross, Simon
Terrill, John Betts, Steven Chee, Gavin Green,
Laurence Bolhaar, Marie-Luise Skibbe,
Timothy Burgess.

DESIGN AND CONSTRUCTION

MPAVILION 2014
Architect: Sean Godsell Architects
Team: Sean Godsell, Hayley Franklin,
    Dayne Trower
Structural engineer: Winward, WSP Melbourne
Builder: Kane Constructions
Lighting: bluebottle
Building surveyor: Nelson McDermott

MPAVILION 2015
Architect: AL_A
Team: Amanda Levete CBE, Alex Bulygin
Structural engineer: ARUP
Builder: Kane Constructions
Specialist fabricator: ShapeShift Technologies
Building surveyor: Gardener Group
Landscape designer: Paul Bangay Garden Design
Lighting: bluebottle, Philips
Audio: Speak Percussion

MPAVILION 2016
Architect: Studio Mumbai
Team: Bijoy Jain, Mitul Desai, Mimo Shirazi
Structural engineer: ARUP
Builder: Kane Constructions
Building surveyor: Gardner Group
Landscape architect: Tract Consulting
Lighting: bluebottle
Audio: Geoffrey Nees with David Franzke
    in collaboration with Aneesh Pradhan

MPAVILION 2017
Architect: OMA
Team: Rem Koolhaas, David Gianotten,
    Paul Jones, Laurence Bolhaar,
    Miguel Taborda, Eve Hocheng,
    Fedor Medek
Structural engineer: ARUP
Builder: Kane Constructions
Specialist fabricator: Kinetic Sets
Building surveyor: Gardner Group
Landscape architect: Tract Consulting
Lighting: bluebottle
Audio: Philip Brophy

MPAVILION 2018
Architect: Estudio Carme Pinós
Team: Carme Pinós, Holger Hennefarth
Architect of record: Leanne Zilka,
    Zilka Studios
Structural engineer: Perrett Simpson
Builder: Kane Constructions
Building surveyor: Gardner Group
Fire engineer: Norman Disney Young
Landscape architect: Tract Consulting
Lighting: bluebottle
Audio: Lisa Greenaway

MPAVILION 2019
Architect: Glenn Murcutt
Team: Glenn Murcutt AO, Jonathan Temple,
    Temple Architecture
Structural engineer: AECOM
Builder: Kane Constructions
Specialist fabricator: Pattons
3D modelling: Julian Featherston
Building surveyor: Gardner Group
Landscape architect: Tract Consulting
Lighting: bluebottle, JSB Lighting

PHOTOGRAPHY

Photographs © the photographers 2020

The photographers/copyright owners
(MPavilion is abbreviated MP and Naomi
Milgrom Foundation is abbreviated NMF):
T: Top/B: Bottom/R: Right/L: Left/C: Centre/
L: Line 1, 2, 3, 4, 5

Adele Varcoe: p. 234 R L1, Alan Weedon:
p. 4, p. 14–15, p. 214 RT, 214 C, p. 217 LB,
p. 235 L L5, p. 238 R L2, Alex Cuffe: p. 215
TC, Amelia Stanwix: p. 234 R L3, Anthony
Richardson: p. 219, Bec Capp: p. 5, p. 7, p. 29,
p. 215 C, 215 CR, 216, p. 217 LT, p. 244–246,
p. 248–249, p. 252, p. 256–257, Benjamin
Huseby: p. 236 C L2, Bri Hammond: p. 238 C
L5, Bryony Jackson: p. 235 C L5, Christelle
Faucoulanche: p. 209 LB, Clara Slewa: p. 238
C L3, Dianna Snape: p. 234 R L4, p. 236 C L4,
Dirk Meinecke: P 237 L L5, Eamon Gallagher:
p. 237 R L3, Earl Carter: p. 52–63, Ed Reeve:
p. 238 R L3, Filip Konikowski: p. 209 C, p. 253,
Gavin Green: p. 132–133, Igor Sapina: p. 237
R L1, Jasmine Blom: p. 239 R L4, p. 239 R L5,
Jeff Busby: p. 237 R L5, Jeremy Weihrauch:
p. 208 C, p. 208 CB, John Betts: p. 9, p. 31,
p. 38–43, p. 209 RB, p. 211 RT, p. 211 LB,
p. 214 LB, p. 215 LB, John Gollings: p. 30,
p. 158–161, John O'Rourke: p. 235 L L2,
Jonnine Standish: p. 235 C L2, Kate Ballis:
p. 237 R L2, Kate Berry: p. 236 C L2, Keelan
O'Hehir: p. 215 LT, p. 234 L L5, Kristina
Kingston: p. 235 R L3, Lars Krüger: p. 234
C L5, Laurence Bolhaar: p. 131, Lee Grant:
p. 237 L L3, Liquid Architecture: p. 211 C,
Marie–Luise Skibbe: p. 163–169, p. 217 RT,
Martin Reddy: p. 209 RT, MP: p. 2–3, p. 6,
p. 10–11, p. 64–65, p. 118–119, p. 170–171,
p. 208–219, p. 250, p. 254, p. 210 RC, p. 210
RB, p. 211 RB, p. 214 BC, p. 217 RC, p. 234
R L1, p. 234 L L2, p. 234 C L2, p. 234 R L2,
p. 234 L L3, p. 234 C L3, p. 234 R L5, p. 235
L L1, p. 235 C L1, p. 235 R L1, p. 235 R L2,
p. 235 L L3, p. 235 C L3, p. 235 C L4, p. 235
R L5, p. 236 C L1, p. 236 R L1, p. 236 L L2,
p. 236 L L3, p. 236 C L3, p. 236 R L3, p. 236
R L4, p. 236 L L4, p. 236, L L5, p. 236, C L5,
p. 236, R L5, p. 237 C L1, p. 237 L L2, p. 237
C L2, p. 237 L L4, p. 237 C L4, p. 237 R L4,
p. 237 L L5, p. 237 C L5, p. 238 L L1, p. 238
C L1, p. 238 R L1, p. 238 L L2, p. 238 L L3,
p. 238 L L4, p. 238 C L4, p. 238 L L5, p. 238
R L5, Nicholas Walker: p. 235 L L4, Nicholas
Watt: p. 91–93, NMF: p. 36, p. 234–239, p. 239
C L1, p. 239 R L1, p. 239 L L2, p. 239 C L2,
p. 239 R L2, p. 239 L L3, p. 239 L L3, p. 239
C L3, p. 239 R L3, p. 239 L L4, p. 239 C L4,
p. 239 L L5, p. 239 C L5, Oslo Davis: p. 237
C L3, Paul Philipson: p. 238 R L4, Richard
Powers: p. 72, p. 210 T, Rory Gardiner: p. 35,
p. 73–83, p. 106–117, p. 179–191, Sarah
Pannell: p. 238 C L2, Sarah Walker: p. 235
R L4, Simon Terrill: p. 194–203, Tom Ross:
p. 142–151, p. 208 RT, p. 223–232, p. 239 L L1,
Stephanie Bakas: p. 218 L, Steven Chee: p. 20,
Timothy Burgess: p. 8, p. 12–13, p. 23, p. 34,
p. 126–127, p. 134–139, p. 218 C, p. 218 B,
p. 234 L L4, p. 234 C L4, p. 239 R L2, p. 247,
p. 251, p. 255, p. 258–259, Tobias Titz: p. 236 L
L1, Tom Jamieson: p. 237 L L1

All the best efforts were made to contact the
rights holders for the images that appear in this
book. Any errors or omissions will be corrected
in future editions.

MPAVILION PRINCIPAL PARTNERS
City of Melbourne, Victorian State Government
through Creative Victoria and Development
Victoria, ANZ, RACV.

MPAVILION SUPPORTERS
Government of Australia, The Embassy of
the Kingdom of the Netherlands, British
Consulate General, Consulate General of
India, Consulate General of Spain, Australian
Council for the Arts, British Council, QIC
GRE, Deloitte Private, Kay & Burton, Arnold
Bloch Leibler, Vic Health, ias Fine Art Logistics,
University of Melbourne, RMIT University,
Monash University, Swinburne University of
Technology, Latrobe University, Arts Centre
Melbourne, Australian Centre for Moving
Image, Melbourne Recital Centre, University
of New South Wales, State Library Victoria,
Community Hubs, Multicultural Arts Victoria,
Australian Institute of Architects, Melbourne
Theatre Company, Open House Melbourne,
Robin Boyd Foundation, Lord Mayor's
Charitable Foundation, Hugh D. T. Williamson
Foundation, Helen Macpherson Smith Trust,
Deborah Cheetham AO, Debbie Dadon AM,
Angie Scanlon, Gandel Philanthropy, Nelson
Meers Foundation, Scanlon Foundation,
Crown Resorts Foundation, Gordon Darling
Foundation, John Truscott Design Foundation,
Renouf & Associates, Copyright Agency
Cultural Fund, Spotless, Studio Ongarato,
Hellenic Museum, Zoos Victoria, Melbourne
International Arts Festival, Confluence: Festival
of India in Australia, Scanlan Theodore, Coleby
Consulting, Two Feathers, Paul Bangay Garden
Design, Bamstone, ACE Contractors Group,
Otway Precast, Britton Timbers, Auswest
Timbers, Laminex, Space Furniture, Assemble
Papers, The Good Copy, Takt Studio, Penso,
Yamaha, Optus, Tin & Ed, Harpy Film Services,
Federation Square, Sofitel Melbourne.

MPAVILION INFORMATION
www.mpavilion.org
www.naomimilgromfoundation.org
Instagram and Twitter: @mpavilion @nmf_au
Facebook.com/mpavilion
Youtube.com/user/mpavilionmelbourne
Vimeo.com/nmfau

MPavilion: Encounters with Design
and Architecture

First published in Australia in 2020
by Thames & Hudson Australia Pty Ltd
11 Central Boulevard
Portside Business Park
Port Melbourne, Victoria 3207
ABN: 72 004 751 964

www.thamesandhudson.com.au

© Naomi Milgrom Foundation 2020

Thames & Hudson Australia wishes to
acknowledge that Aboriginal and Torres Strait
Islander people are the first storytellers of
this nation and the traditional custodians
of the land on which we live and work. We
acknowledge their continuing culture and pay
respect to Elders past, present and future.

978-1-76076-056-4

NATIONAL
LIBRARY
OF AUSTRALIA

A catalogue record for this work is available
from the National Library of Australia.

Every effort has been made to trace accurate
ownership of copyrighted text and visual
materials used in this book. Errors or omissions
will be corrected in subsequent editions,
provided notification is sent to the publisher.

Foreword: Naomi Milgrom AO
Contributors: Stephen Todd, Dame Julia Peyton-
    Jones DBE, Rory Hyde, Aric Chen, Ellie
    Stathaki, Caroline Roux,
    Françoise Fromonot
Editors: Alexandra Zafiriou, Robert Buckingham
Publisher: Kirsten Abbott
Design and art direction: Studio Ongarato
Copy editor: Adam Curley
Research: Isabella Woolcott

Printed and bound in China by Everbest.